Doo-WopCentrism*

The Top 2000 Doo-Wop Songs

by Anthony J. Gribin
& Matthew M. Schiff

*Doo-WopCentrism, n. [from Amer. doo-wop, great music, and center, and -ism.] the firmly held belief that vocal group rhythm and blues, created between the late 1940s and early 1960s, is vastly superior to all other musics, with no exceptions. Got it?
-Websters Unabridged Dictionary (not)

ttgPress

ISBN-13: 978-0-9827376-7-5

ttgPress

This Book is dedicated to YouTube

Related Books by These Authors:

Doo-Wop: The Forgotten Third of Rock & Roll (Gribin & Schiff, 1992)

The Complete Book of Doo-Wop (Gribin & Schiff, 2000. Reissued 2009)

Who Sang Our Songs? (Friedman & Gribin, 2005)

The Encyclopedia Of Early American Vocal Groups: 100 Years Of Harmony - 1850-1950 (Friedman & Gribin, 2013)

The Top 1000 Doo-Wop Songs: Collector's Edition (Gribin & Schiff, 2014)

Unrelated Books by These Authors:

You're Not Nuts... You've Just Got Issues (Gribin, 2006)

For Parents & Teens: A Guide To Peaceful Coexistence (Gribin, 2007)

Them There Guys: An E-pistolary Odyssey (Gribin & Finkelstein, 2010)

Selfonomics: How Broadly-Defined Self-Interest Explains Every thing (Gribin, 2013)

Road Trip: Europe 1967 (Gribin, 2014)

Table of Contents

Acknowledgments

In response to our "HELP WANTED" plea in the postscript of "The Top 1000 Doo-Wop Songs: Collector's Edition, we relied on three sources: our own heads, the suggestions of other lovers of the music, and the postings of avid fans on either YouTube, Facebook or both.

Thanking ourselves seems rather silly, so instead we'd like to thank everyone else. With appreciation to (among others) 4JUKEBOXSATURDAYNITE, Amnondoowop, Marty B, Mickey Bo, James Devlin, Joe DiMaria, Bennie Dingo, "DooWop Paradise," David Finkelstein, Doug Friedman, Larry Ginsberg, Stu Grossman, Paul S. Gruber, Dorothy Horstmann, Joe Landau, Olli Leben, Frank Miller, Dennis Marcucci, TheNickNicola, P.J. Noce (PJDoo-Wop), Tony O, Jackie Wasserman Perl, Wayne Smith, Alan David Stein, Nils Yngvar Stenstad, Jack Strong, doktorsung, Phil Unger, and Gary Zaretsky. These people either suggested songs to be included in the Top 2000, or were gracious enough to share their music on YouTube so that we could pluck out the best of their goodies...

Introduction

There's a reason that this book is dedicated to "YouTube." Even though we authors have listened to doo-wop for years on radio, records and CDs, it was impossible to reach all the outliers; the songs that were less popular and/or available. YouTube changed all that. Combined with other internet sites such as Facebook, YouTube has enabled the possibility of looking up ("googling") titles and artists, and the sharing of record and track collections. The formal name of this act is "crowdsourcing," which for music at least, can be traced back to Napster, a peer-to-peer music sharing service which operated for a few years starting in 1999. The upshot is that anyone with a computer or smart phone can hear just about any doo-wop song they want. As long as they know what to look for that is, which brings us to the purpose of this book.

In 2014, we published a book entitled "The Top 1000 Doo-Wop Songs: Collector's Edition." At its end, our postscript advertised "Help Wanted!" so that we could continue to unearth more doo-wop gems. Though many of the second thousand were already familiar to us, approximately 350 were unknown. By taking suggestions from people mentioned in the "Acknowledgments" and by listening to the offerings of doo-wop enthusiasts who regularly post their collections on YouTube, we were able to amass another thousand favorites.

A note on the choice of songs that were included in the second thousand. We'll offer a baseball analogy. If one hundred baseball fans were asked to list their Top Twenty position players over the history of baseball, almost all would include Babe Ruth, Henry Aaron, Ted Williams, Jackie Robinson, Mickey Mantle, Willie Mays, Joe DiMaggio and Ty Cobb. There might be some disagreement over who would fill out the top twenty, but most of the choices would be understandable. If someone had Stan Musial on his list and another had Albert Pujols or

Roberto Clemente, no one would raise an eyebrow. But what if we asked for the Top Forty? Our guess would be that there would be a lot more variation in the chosen players. Cincinnati Red fans would probably include Joe Morgan, Pete Rose and Johnny Bench, while Yankee fans would include Lou Gehrig, Derek Jeter and Yogi Berra. Younger fans might want to include Jeter, Miguel Cabrera and Mike Trout, middle aged fans would favor Frank Robinson, George Brett and Ozzie Smith, and older fans would vote for Tris Speaker, Honus Wagner and Rogers Hornsby. The larger the number of players selected the more disagreement there would be, and the factors determining ones choice would have a lot to do with age and where one grew up. (In the field of psychology, it would be said that the "inter-rater agreement" would be lower for the larger number of players chosen.)

It's the same when choosing doo-wop songs to be included in a list. The Top 1000 includes "musts" such as the Holy Trinity ("In The Still of the Night" by the Five Satins, "Earth Angel" by the Penguins and "Tonite Tonite" by the Mello-Kings), and chestnuts such as "I Wonder Why" by Dion & the Belmonts, "Sincerely" by the Moonglows, "Close Your Eyes" by the Five Keys, "Crazy For You" by the Heartbeats and "Tell Me Why" by Norman Fox & the Rob Roys. Anyone who thinks these songs should not be included in the Top 1000 is certifiably nuts. To round out the Top 1000, we chose the major hits by the major groups, the one-hit wonders (such as "Cora Lee" by Little Bobby Rivera and the Hemlocks and "Bermuda Shorts" by the Delroys) and several tracks by many semi-famous groups such as the Four Fellows, Collegians and Mello-Moods. After collecting all of these, there was also a little room for favorites of the authors, such as "You've Been Gone" by the Fabulous Pearl Devines and "And When I'm Near You" by Richie & the Royals. But most songs included in the Top 1000 just had to be there.

In choosing our second thousand songs, we included some very well-known tracks that just couldn't be included in the Top 1000, for want of space. The first source of the second thousand was drilling down deeper into the bodies of work of famous groups. For example, the first Drifters group (which featured Clyde McPhatter) placed twelve songs on the Top 1000, to which were added seven more in the second thousand. The second Drifters group (featuring Ben E. King) placed five songs in the Top 1000 and eight more when the list was expanded to 2000 songs. Other examples are "Over And Over Again" by the Moonglows which was left off the first 1000 because we favored nine other Moonglows songs, and "Annie Had A Baby" by Hank Ballard & the Midnighters, omitted because we already had "Work With Me Annie" and "Sexy Ways" in the first 1000.

A second source of "new" songs were actual "newer" recordings. The Top 1000 included only 5 songs included that were recorded after 1964. In the Top 2000, an additional 146 songs were added from after the era. Many of this large number were recorded by post-era super groups such as the Legends of Doo-Wop, Kenny Vance & the Planetones, the Sheps, Choice and Valentinos, as well as some "upstart" younger groups such as the Earth Angels and Roomates who hail from Spain and England respectively.

A third source of additional songs was allowing the inclusion of more than one version of great songs. The Jewels version of "Hearts Of Stone" appeared in the Top 1000, and the version by Otis Williams & the Charms was left out. The Top 2000 allowed inclusion of both. Though Jimmy Castor & the Juniors had the first version of "I Promise To Remember," we left it out of the Top 1000 in favor of the Teenagers version. Both appear in the Top 2000. Since there is more "room" in the Top 2000, acappella versions of non-acappella songs have been added; to wit, the Passions' "I Only Want You" was done acappella by Richie & the Royals in 1963 and the Passions' "This Is My Love," retitled "Sweeter Than" and performed acappella by the Young Ones in 1964. These multiple versions allow the reader (and listener) to compare them by playing them sequentially. Suggestions for many comparisons are offered towards the end of this book.

A fourth source of songs is the "B sides" of hits included in the Top 1000. Examples are "Without You," the flip of "Life Is But A Dream" by the Earls, "Please Be Mine," flip of "Why Do Fools Fall In Love" by Frankie Lymon & the Teenagers and "You Never Loved Me," the B-side of "Book Of Love" by the Monotones.

A fifth source of entries are songs that were performed by artists usually not associated with the doo-wop genre. Thus the Top 2000 contains tracks by Little Eva ("Locomotion"), Jimmy Jones ("Handy Man"), Gene Pitney ("Darkness"), David Gates (with the Accents on "What's This I Hear"), Bo Diddley ("I'm Sorry") and Little Richard ("True Fine Mama") among others. All of these songs were recorded with a group in the background and thus meet the requirements of the definition of doo-wop.

And then there are the oddball, one-off hits that are impossible to not appreciate, though they are not likely to have been chosen by a different set of authors in their own Top 2000. Included in this category are "Please Come Back" by the Mon-Claires, "Dum Dum De Dip" by Judy & the Affections, "Singing Bells" by the Off-Keys (definitely a misnomer) and "Vines Of Love" by the Del Rios. These are all great songs, but unknown to many doo-wop fans.

What Is Doo-Wop Music?

This section was copied directly from The Top 1000 Doo-Wop Songs: Collector's Edition. The purpose is to orient those readers who are not veteran doo-wop fans to the subject matter at hand.

The reader might ask, "What makes doo-wop more important than other genres of music, such as Big Band, British rock, heavy metal, grunge or alternative?" While all of these types of music will have nostalgia value for those who grew up with them, doo-wop sets itself apart psychologically.

Both authors are mental health professionals and are aware of the characteristics of adults who are happy as they become mature. For example, we all value love and relationships. We all seek to be happy in our lives and find pastimes that are familiar and soothing as a respite from our stress-laden lives. We all like things to be predictable and we strive for closure; that is, we don't like unfinished business. We also value getting along, living in harmony and mellowing out as the years pass. Doo-wop lets us do these things better than other types of music.

While all genres will provide fond memories of youth and young love to a middle aged (or older) person, doo-wop deals exclusively with young love as its subject matter. Exceptions are rare. Doo-wop is basically a happy, innocent music. There is little discord either in the lyrics or the melodies. Most doo-wops make you smile. Not think deeply or support a cause; just smile and maybe sing along.

The melodies, with their four-chord progressions, always seem familiar and soothing. In a way, that's a knock against the music; that it is too repetitive in its melodies and its "by my side to be my guide/bride" lyrics. But along with repetition comes familiarity and comfort. We know these songs in our gut; we can often start humming one and end up singing another. Because many of them are similar, they blend.

Finally, the blending of voices that produces the harmony of doo-wop is a parable for the rest of life. Just as the singers blend and work together, so do we strive to "go along to get along." We now turn to the characteristics of the music we love.

The doo-wop style requires that there be at least three people singing. Two people don't count even when the arrangement sounds doo-woppy, as in songs by Marvin & Johnny, Johnny & Joe, Robert & Johnny and Don & Juan. We call that "duo-wop." There are also songs that sound doo-woppy and that are performed by single artists, such as "Angel Baby" by Rosie & the Originals and "Love You So" by Ron Holden & the Thunderbirds. The songs have a doo-wop feel, tempo and doo-wop-friendly group name, but there's no vocal group. That's "uni-wop." For those of you who think we are taking our subject lightly, you are correct. This is a fun music and we intend to enjoy it thoroughly whether writing about or listening to it.

The usual group is comprised of four members, but five is common (three and six less so). Aside from the lead in a quartet, usually a tenor, a second tenor and baritone blend to produce background harmony, and there is a bass voice that either joins the harmonizers or sings a separate bass line under the harmony. When five are present, there are three harmonizers, a lead and a bass. Sometimes a tenor will float above the lead in falsetto.

Another characteristic of doo-wop, present more often than not, is the presence of nonsense syllables, such as "bon bon," bum bah bum," "tra la la" or "doo-wop." They are usually uttered by the bass, but can be sung by the harmonizers as well. Their frequency of use increased as the doo-wop era unfurled, to the point where their presence often became the focus of a song at the end of the era (examples are "Blue Moon" by the Marcels and most uptempo songs by the Earls).

Other common features of the genre are simple music and lyrics and light instrumentation except during the bridge (middle) of the song, when a sax often wails or a piano tinkles. The subject matter is almost invariably about young love, lost, found or desired from afar. It is a happy, joyful, harmonic and youthful music produced by a culture in relative harmony. It is a music by young people for young people and does not deal with the hardships of life as would the musics of later eras.

We've divided the era, which spans roughly 1948 to 1963, into three parts. "Paleo-Doo-Wop" runs from 1948 to 1954. Almost all of these early songs are by black groups. White singers hadn't entered the picture yet. Paleo- songs featured plaintive, sometimes operatic leads featuring soulful voices that often got their start singing gospel in church. The nonsense syllables employed were simple and infrequent (doh doh doh). The groups were comprised of older, more mature singers and sometimes the lyrics were lascivious ("It Ain't the Meat" by the Swallows and "Sixty Minute Man" by the Dominoes).

The Classical-Doo-Wop era (1955-1959) saw the entry of very young teens to the fray (Frankie Lymon, Pearl McKinnon) featuring high tenor "schoolboy" leads in 1955. A few years later white groups made the charts beginning with the white led, mixed race groups such as the Crests and Norman Fox & the Rob Roys, and then all-white groups like Danny & the Juniors, the Elegants and Dion & the Belmonts. Melodies and lyrics were simple and innocent, and nonsense syllables more pronounced. Falsetto was common, often used as a trail-off at the end of the song, and the bass line became more prominent.

The third period, Neo-Doo-Wop ran roughly from 1960-1963. This was the era of the "Oldies But Goodies" sound, that brought the old slow sounds to a new generation of teens. Being young, this new generation was attracted to glitzy exaggerations of the fast Classical sound. The bassi and falsetti were prominent, often leading a song, which occurred only rarely in the Classical time frame. Old slow songs were remade uptempo (e.g. "Blue Moon," "Life Is But A Dream" and "The Closer You Are"). Tin Pan Alley composers joined the mix and

15

instrumentation increased. A chart describing doo-wop characteristics through the years follows:

Doo-Wop Characteristics in Different Time Periods

	Pre-DW (before '48)	Paleo-DW ('48-'54)	Classical DW ('55-'59)	Neo-DW ('60-'63)	Post-DW (after '63)
Non-sense Sylls.	not present or used in different ways	emergence blow harmonies & simple patterns of non. sylls.	more complex patterns in almost every song	subdued in some cases and more complex patterns in others	words replace non. sylls. as background responses
Harmony Part	humming very much in background	given more voice may alternate with lead	given even more voice	same as classical	recedes into background
Falsetto	occasionally present but has operatic quality	present more often occasionally leads, operatic quality	almost always present, frequently leads, almost always used as trail-off	not always present but more freq. leads when present, used less as trail-off	diminished presence, almost never leads or used as trail-off
Bass	freq. bass leads and talking bridges, but not between stanzas not distinct from harmony	begins to separate from harmony, begins to punctuate stanzas	frequently introduces song, almost always separate from harmony by punctuating or riffing	same as classical, but sometimes used in exaggerated ways	used less as separate voice throughout
Beat	allied with jazz, r&b or other earlier styles	very little jazz influence, more allied with r&b	beat heavy & distinct (on 2nd & 4th beats), allied with rock & roll	same as classical except for pop-DW softer beat	remains heavy in most new musics

	Pre-DW (before '48)	Paleo-DW ('48-'54)	Classical DW ('55-'59)	Neo-DW ('60-'63)	Post-DW (after '63)
Instru-ments	heavier than standard doo-wop fare	less present than before, honky-tonk piano or organ typical	instruments unimportant except during break in mid-dle of song	instruments re-emerging	instruments much more important
Melody	blues or jazz progressions	melodies begin to simplify	simple melodies & four-chord structures common	more variation than in classical	significantly more variation in melodies
Lyrics	often lascivious in r&b, else mature love themes	still lascivious but innocent love themes begin to take over	almost exclusively innocent love, almost no politi-cizing or social commentary	lyrics remain innocent	most lyrics still deal with love, but social com-mentary & politicizing appears

17

About the Top 2000

Distribution of Songs by Year

The bar chart immediately below represents the Top 1000 songs. Notice the bimodal distribution, with peaks in 1957 and 1961, representing Classical Doo-Wop and Neo-Doo-Wop respectively.

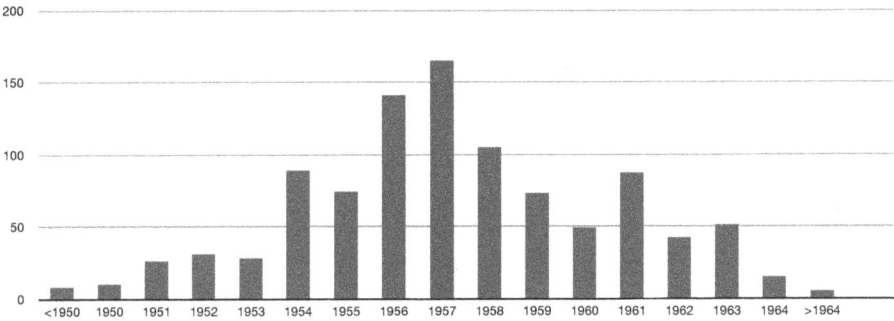

The second bar chart shows how the second thousand songs are distributed. There are peaks at 1958 representing Classical Doo-Wop and a huge peak at 1961 for Neo-Doo-Wop, implying that the second thousand songs are slightly more skewed to later songs than the first 1000. Also note the huge bump in the after-1964 category which indicates that we have chosen many post-era groups and their songs to be included in the second thousand.

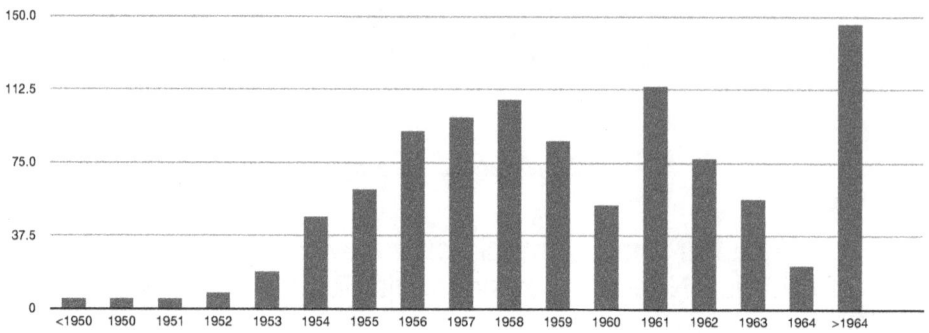

The third chart is merely a combination of the first two; that is, the overall distribution of the Top 2000 songs. Again, peaks at 1957 and 1961, with an extra bump on the end for newer, post-era releases.

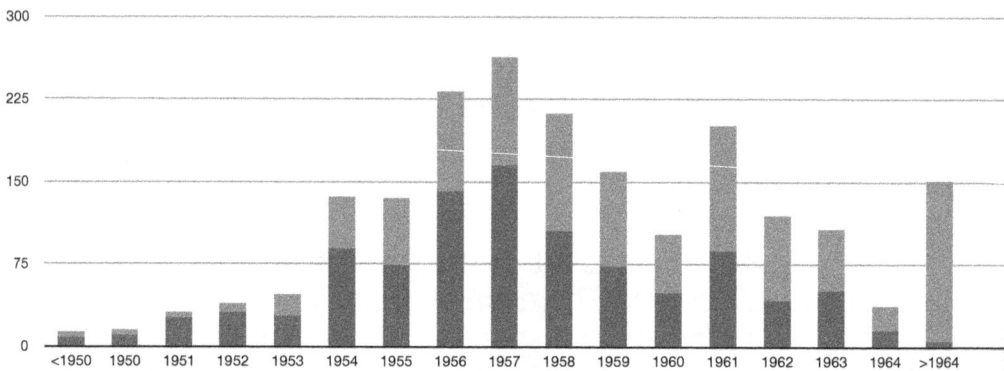

Distribution of Songs by Era and Tempo

      Overall, there were more slow than fast songs in the Top 2000 (1121 to 838). The first thousand has many more Paleo- songs and less Neo- songs than in the second thousand.

      More songs came from the Classical era (1158) than from the Neo- era (466) or the Paleo- era (376). The second thousand songs were more concentrated in the Classical era than the first thousand (637 to 521). There were more fast songs and less slow songs in the second thousand than in the first thousand. Medium tempo songs are mostly cha-chas and may be slightly underrepresented.

First 1000 Songs

	Paleo-DW	Classical DW	Neo-DW	Sum
Slow	230	270	85	585
Medium	1	6	17	24
Fast	43	245	103	391
Sum	274	521	205	1000

Second 1000 Songs

	Paleo-DW	Classical DW	Neo-DW	Sum
Slow	71	371	94	536
Medium	0	9	8	17
Fast	31	257	159	447
Sum	102	637	261	1000

2000 Songs Combined

Sum	Paleo-DW	Classical DW	Neo-DW	
Slow	301	641	179	1121
Medium	1	15	25	41
Fast	74	502	262	838
Sum	376	1158	466	2000

Groups That Appear the Most Often

A list of the total of 95 groups that placed five or more songs in the Top 2000 appears below, and these 95 groups accounted for 809 of the 2000 songs (40.45%).

Of the 95 groups, 18 (18.9%) are predominantly white and represent 123 of the 809 songs (15.2%) and 77 (81.1%) are of color and produced 686 (84.8%) of the Top 2000. Nineteen out of the top 20 groups are black, the Earls being the one exception.

Five of the 95 (5.3%) groups were predominantly female and 4 more (4.2%) were male groups led by females. The predominantly female groups contributed 37 of the 809 songs by the 95 groups, or 4.6%, while the female-led male groups sang 23 or 809, or 2.8%. So males made up 86 of 95 groups, or 90.5% and contributed 748 of 809, or 92.5% of the songs.

	First Top 1000	Second Top 1000	Sum
Drifters (B)	12	7	19
Cadillacs	10	6	16
Cleftones	7	9	16
Flamingos	11	5	16
Platters	12	4	16
Harptones	10	5	15
Spaniels	8	7	15
Clovers	9	5	14
Earls	6	8	14
Five Keys	11	3	14
Hearts, Lee Andrews &	9	5	14
Moonglows	9	5	14
Nutmegs	9	5	14
Solitaires	11	3	14
Teenagers, F. Lymon &	9	5	14
Channels, Earl Lewis &	7	6	13
Crowns, A. L .Maye &	5	8	13

Diablos (& Velvet Angels)	6	7	13
Drifters (C)	5	8	13
Heartbeats	9	4	13
Orioles	9	4	13
Crests	8	4	12
Dominoes	10	2	12
Ravens	8	4	12
Shirelles	7	5	12
Coasters	7	3	10
Hi-Lites (B)	2	8	10
Legends Of Doo-Wop	0	10	10
DiMucci, Dion (& group)	3	6	9
Imperials (B), Anthony &	6	3	9
Jesters	8	1	9
Mystics (A)	6	3	9
Rob Roys, Norman Fox &	5	4	9
Belmonts, Dion & the	5	4	9
Chantels	3	5	8
Chanters	4	4	8
Five Satins	6	2	8
Hurricanes	4	4	8
Marcels	3	5	8
Paragons	7	1	8
Swallows	7	1	8
Teenchords, L. Lymon &	5	3	8
Cardinals	6	1	7
Castelles	5	2	7
Charms	5	2	7
Chiffons	4	3	7
Crows	5	2	7
Dell Vikings	5	2	7
Dells	5	2	7
Dubs	5	2	7
El Dorados	6	1	7
Five Discs	5	2	7
Four Buddies	5	2	7
Four Fellows	6	1	7
Jive Five	4	3	7

Mellows, Lillian Leach &	5	2	7
Shells	3	4	7
Bop-Chords	5	1	6
Capris (B)	3	3	6
Charts	5	1	6
Checkers	3	3	6
Imaginations	3	3	6
Juniors (B), Danny & the	3	3	6
Keynotes	3	3	6
King Crooners	3	3	6
Kodaks	4	2	6
Larks (A)	5	1	6
Pearls (+Five Pearls)	2	4	6
Penguins	4	2	6
Planetones, Kenny Vance &	0	6	6
Spiders	5	1	6
Time-Tones	3	3	6
Angels (B)	2	3	5
Choice	0	5	5
Continentals (A)	5	0	5
Crystals	3	2	5
Darchaes	1	4	5
Duprees	4	1	5
Earth Angels	0	5	5
El Venos	0	5	5
Eternals	3	2	5
G-Clefs	4	1	5
Hollywood (Four) Flames	3	2	5
Passions	3	2	5
Schoolboys	3	2	5
Sensations	3	2	5
Sheps	0	5	5
Skyliners	5	0	5
Students	3	2	5
Tokens (B)	2	3	5
Turbans	3	2	5
Valentines	4	1	5
Valentinos	0	5	5

Vocaleers	3	2	5
Wrens	3	2	5
Sum:	480	329	809

The 1st Doctor of Doo-Wop

In 1992, after a two year process, Matt Schiff and I finished and published "Doo-Wop: The Forgotten Third Of Rock 'n' Roll." We had a "singing and signing" at a local bookstore (remember those?) and hired a group called the Shoretones, to entertain and attract passersby. We billed ourselves as "The Doctors of Doo-Wop," since one of us is a Ph.D. and the other is an M.D. We appeared as such on radio shows such as Don K. Reed's "Doo-Wop Shop" and Ronnie Italiano's "R&B Party" soon afterwards. Several others with doctoral or medical degrees chose to use the Doctor of Doo-Wop handle, but we were pretty sure we were the first. Not so fast...

Just recently we learned that the moniker had been used before though we don't know whether he claimed it or it was ascribed to him by someone else. His name was Dave Antrell, and from the little we know of him, he was a physician who was active in the music business, most successfully as a composer and recorder of the old sounds, from around 1985 to 1990. His labels were called Antrell and Classic Artists Recordings, and he assembled a host of old groups, in full or in part, to record new songs that he wrote for them, occasionally with co-composers.

Since we have allowed ourselves to choose our second 1000 recordings from any time period, we have chosen to include many of these recordings, including:

Blue Jays, Leon Peels & the	Once Upon A Love
Blue Jays, Leon Peels & the	Alice From Above
Channels, Earl Lewis & the	Do What Lovers Do
Cleftones, Herb Cox & the	My Angel Lover
Cleftones, Herb Cox & the	You Lost The Game Of Love
Dubs, Richard Blandon & the	Wherever You Are
Five Boroughs	Heaven And Cindy
Jaguars (feat. Val Poliuto)	Play A Love Song
Maye, Arthur Lee (& group)	Moonlight

Maye, Arthur Lee (& group)	Happy And In Love
Storytellers	Please Remember My Love
Storytellers	Heaven's For Real (A. Sanchez)
Tune Weavers, Margo Sylvia &	Come Back To Me (R. Saunders)
Tune Weavers, Margo Sylvia &	What Are You Doing New Year's Eve (F. Loesser)

Doc Antrell wrote all of the above, aside from the last three whose composers appear in parentheses, but he had a hand in producing all of them. The neat part, if you are a fan of the genre, is that all the songs are written in the style of the group that recorded them. That is, the Blue Jays' songs fit nicely into the body of work that they recorded within the doo-wop era (roughly 1948-1963).

The listed tracks are available on YouTube. If you prefer to own them, most of the above can be heard on two CDs from 1989-1990, entitled "Doo-Wop Diner, Vols. 1 & 2" from Classic Artists Recordings, that can be bought on eBay and other re-sellers. Many of Antrell's songs can also be found on a CD called "Classic Doo-Wop," put out in 1993 by Classic Artists Recordings in conjunction with Ace Records.

Calling Antrell a genius may be a stretch, but not by much. His compositions and recordings made many people very happy, in the same way as new Sherlock Holmes stories, written by lovers of Conan Doyle, and new James Bond novels written by John Gardner have always been eagerly anticipated by fans. These songs are really, really good.

As the last testimony to Antrell's talent, he recorded over himself four times as the Five Arcades in 1973 on the ballad "Hoping You'll Fall In Love," which is included in the Top 2000. The flip is called "Buy A Van," by Little Flaytus & the Dream-Airs, which we considered not worthy of inclusion. But Doc Antrell, posing as Little Flaytus, couldn't help showing off his medical chops: flatus is a term for gas expelled from one's nether region.

Doc Antrell died too young.

Artists Who Found Fame In Other Genres

When compiling the Top 1000, we felt compelled to select the best, most popular and most representative songs of the era. That mission meant that we had to omit some very interesting tracks on the margins of doo-wop, recorded both during and after the era. One interesting category of songs left out were recorded by artists who made their mark at different times and in different genres. By expanding our goal to the Top 2000 songs, many of these tracks can now be included. Songs that were added in the second thousand appear in **bold type**.

To begin, consider the rhythm & blues of Bo Diddley, Varetta Dillard, Little Richard and Huey Smith & the Clowns. We've included "**I'm Sorry**" by Diddley & group from 1959, a four-chord plaintive ballad with a group singing "ooh wee ooh, wop wop" in the background. Dillard recorded "**Darling, Listen To The Words Of This Song**," backed by the Four Students in 1956, a year after Ruth McFadden's version backed by the Supremes (a Bronx group featuring Waldo Champen) was released. Dillard's version is different, but equally as good. Compare the two versions and come to your own conclusion.

Then, use YouTube to listen to Little Richard's recording of "**True Fine Mama**," a rocker recorded in 1955 but not released until 1958. A New Orleans funky piano and a call-and-response performance by the backing group has you tapping your feet. Borderline doo-wop, and just plain fun. Smith and the Clowns, known for their New Orleans styled uptempos such as "Don't You Just Know It," also recorded a beautiful ballad called "**Dearest Darling (You're The One)**" which may just surprise you.

Next, many Motown stars began their careers in doo-wop and/or R&B groups. It is rumored that both Marvin Gaye and Billy Stewart was associated with the Rainbows of "Mary Lee" fame as part of their circle of friends, but never recorded with them. The Four Tops recorded in doo-wop style when they began as the Four Aims. Ronnie Spector Bennett was the lead of Ronnie and the Relatives, who recorded "**I Want A Boy**," a song included in our Top 2000. It is a precursor of hits by the Ronettes, but frankly is not as good and certainly not as polished. The Miracles, with Smokey Robinson, but before his name headed the group, produced "**Bad Girl**," in 1959 with a nice smooth doo-wop sound. And the Isley Brothers had an early doo-wop rock 'n' roller in 1957, entitled "**The Cow Jumped Over The Moon**."

Single artists that started with or in doo-wop groups were not unusual. Witness Clyde McPhatter (Dominoes and Drifters), Jackie Wilson (Dominoes), Dion DiMucci (Belmonts), Bobby Darin (Rinky Dinks and Ding Dongs), Carole King (Palisades), Wilson Pickett (Falcons), Frankie Lymon (Teenagers), Teddy Randazzo (Three Chuckles), Neil Sedaka (Tokens), Ben E. King (Five Crowns and the second Drifters group), Phil Spector (Teddy Bears and Spector's Three), Dee Clark (Kool Gents), Bobby Freeman (Romancers), Ernie K-Doe (Blue Diamonds), Van McCoy (Starlighters), Robert John (Bobby & the Consoles) and Brook Benton (Sandmen), not to mention the Motown-related stars previously identified. Many of these artists sang with groups that have multiple songs on the Top 1000.
To this list, the Top 2000 adds Little Eva with "**Locomotion**," Bobby Lewis on "**Tossin' and Turnin'**," Jimmy Jones with the Savoys on "**Say You're Mine**" and with the Cues on "**Handy Man**," Lou Christie as Lugee, of Lugee & the Lions, with "**The Jury**," Gene Pitney fronting the Embers on "**Darkness**," and Joey Dee with the Starliters on "**Lorraine**."

Remember Cannibal & the Headhunters? A garage band that issued the seminal dance tune "Land Of A Thousand Dances"? Well, they recorded a nice ballad in doo-wop style called "**I'll Show You How To Love Me**," in 1965, which is in our Top 2000. And do you recall the soft rock group called "Bread," who had a run of hits in the early 1970s (13 charted on the Billboard Top 100) such as "Baby I'm-A Want You," "Make It With You," and "Everything I Own"? Their lead singer was David Gates who, with the Accents, recorded a precursor to the Bread sound with "**What's This I Hear?**" in 1960. It's a great ballad that's included in our Top 2000.

And then there are the world-famous artists that started stuck their toes in the waters of doo-wop, one way or the other. Listen to two included tracks by the Beach Boys, "**Surfin'**" from 1961 and "**Surfer Girl**" from 1963. The former was the Beach Boys first hit and first surf song, and has a resounding bass line, "bon, bon dip-duh-dip duh-dip." The latter is a sweet ballad replete with background harmony and lilting falsetto.

Frankie Valli made the Top 1000 with the Four Lovers "You're The Apple Of My Eye" from 1956. His strong falsetto voice was his signature and bordered on the doo-wop style. We've included "**Marlena**" in our Top 2000. Paul Simon sang as Jerry Landis (with a group) on "Lone Teen Ranger," briefly with the Mystics on "All Through The Night," and with Tico & the Triumphs on "Cards of Love," all of which in the Top 1000. And finally, Billy Joel overdubbed his own voice for each part of "**The Longest Time**," which made the Top 2000.

Post-Era Groups and Songs

For the first Top 1000, only a few songs after 1964 made the list, the most important of which was arguably "Morse Code Of Love" by the Capris (B). Widening our scope, 146 songs of the second group of 1000 songs come from 1965 and after. They hail from a range of sources, many of which are home-grown, and some of which were born in foreign lands.

Our favorite, at least by the number of songs included in the Top 2000 (ten), are the Legends Of Doo-Wop, consisting of lead singers Tony Passalacqua of the Fascinators, Frank Mancuso of the Imaginations and Jimmy Gallagher of the Passions, plus bass Steve Horn of the Five Sharks. Between them, the Fascinators, Imaginations and Passions had a host of hits, all of which were re-recorded by this super group. They added a few wrinkles (listen to "**Oh Rosemarie**") and still had four very good voices to carry it off. We are definitely in the tank for these guys.

Kenny Vance and the Planetones also did right by our favorite genre, placing six songs in the Top 2000. Vance has a strong, sweet and clear voice and his new arrangements of old songs, especially on ballads such as "**The Way You Look Tonight**" and "**Diamonds and Pearls**" are exquisite. Plus there's his paean to doo-wop, a "new" song (1975) called "**Looking For An Echo**," that describes the lives of singers back in the day, and has become an anthem for our music.

Other groups from after the era include Valentinos (5 songs on the list) including their wonderful version of the Dubs' "Chapel of Dreams" entitled "**I Miei Giorni Felici**" (which means "My Happy Days" in Italian), the Sheps (5), Choice (5), Little Isidore & the Inquisitors (3), Patty & the Street-Tones (3),

33

the Manhattan Transfer (2), Jaynells (2), Lar-Kings (1), Reunion (1), Cliftones (1), and the Doo-Wop All-Stars (1).

Though we're sure that we left many of the readers' favorites off the list, remember what we said at the beginning: that in the second Top 1000 many of the choices are going to be individual preferences.

Finally, in this category, we are happy to note that some of our European friends have joined the bandwagon. There's an acappella group from Spain called the Earth Angels who have a lead with a truly unbelievable voice whose name is Gustavo Castanada. Listen to their rendition of the Lytations' **"Look Into The Sky."** They redo American hits, many of which are just as good as the originals, with a few twists necessary to the acappella style. They placed five songs on our new list.

Placing three songs were the Roomates from England, including a doo-wop version of the Beach Boys' **"Little Miss America"** and the Quotations' **"Alamensay."** Three German groups placed two songs apiece on the list: the Bel-Angels, Crystalairs, and Mysterials. All of the German groups have precise harmony and machine gun bassmen, and they excel on uptempo numbers. The faster the song, the more they step up. Listen to the Crystalairs on **"Ding Dong Teenage Bells,"** the Bel-Airs on **"Teenage Bells"** (these are two versions of the same song originally recorded by the Five Secrets in 1957), and the Mysterials on **"Shambalaya."**

New Gems

In collecting tracks to include in the second thousand, one obvious way to go was to dig deeper into the body of works by well-known groups like the Harptones, the Clyde McPhatter Drifters, Five Keys and Moonglows. Another path was to collect, one by one, "one-and-done" groups whose hard-to-find tracks tickled our fancy, or secondary tracks by almost-famous groups. Listen to them and see if you agree with our taste. If you don't you must be nuts...

Fast

Affections, Judy & the   **Dum Dum De Dip**   1964
A girl group from Harper Woods, MI, with a bouncy, teeny sound. Wish they had put out many more records.

Bees   **Sunny Side Of The Street**   1954
"If I haven't got a cent, I'd be rich as Rocky Fellow (sic)" Fun version, very different.

Chancellors   **There Goes My Girl**   1957
Interracial group from Mineola and Port Washington, NY. Hard beat, New York City sound.

Chips   **Darling I Need Your Love**   1960
Not the "Rubber Biscuit" group. This one is from Cali with a sweet mid-tempo poppish song.

Concepts   **Jungle**   1961
"Jigga Megga Mugga Mugga," or something to that effect. A great "Stranded In The Jungle" type side, with a big bass and rhythm. The nonsense talk is a hoot!

35

Corvells **Take My Love** 1962
   Good Philadelphia rocker.

Del-Chords **Say That You Love Me** 1960
   Soft, pleasant uptempo.

Del-Rays **Around The Corner** 1959
   White group from White Plains, NY.

Del Rios **Vines Of Love** 1958
   "Wear this ring around your finger, as for your thoughts
   (sic, should've been "doubts") they'll no longer linger."
   Texas group with a twang and a peppy song that's tough
   to get out of your head.

Dellchords, D. Campanella & **Everything's That Way** 1959
   David Campanella, adopted son of the Brooklyn Dodgers'
   Roy Campanella, wrote and spoke the famous proto-rap
   riff at the end of the song, though he wasn't on lead.
   He died a drug-related death at 41. Pleasant, soft up-
   tempo. Flip of "Somewhere Over The Rainbow."

Incredible Upsetters **Ooh-Wah-Cha-Wah** 1959
   Frantic rocker with the title of the song as background
   throughout. Group unknown.

Infatuators **I Found My Love** 1961
   One of the authors was in his car about 20 years ago
   and heard the bass riff to this song: "heavy chevy doo-
   wop, omm baby doo-wop." He finally found the track
   about a year ago. Great bass, bridge and flip side!

Mystics **The Bells Are Ringing** 1958
   This is really by the Overons, the Mystics before they
   were Mystics. Great white group sound, melodious and
   well-performed, like all the rest of their body of work.

Off-Keys   **Singing Bells**   1962
> Mellow sound from this Camden, NJ white group. Lead and bass noteworthy. Why is this group unknown?

Trueloves   **A Love Like Yours**   1957
> Schoolboy doo-wop, good bass.

Vocal-Teens   **Be A Slave**   1958
> Jersey City, NJ group with a melodious cha-cha entry.

Wisdoms   **Lost In Dreams**   1959
> Group from Minneapolis, MN, of all places. Sweet lead.

Slow

Accents, David Gates &   **What's This I Hear?**   1960
> Anyone who knows the band Bread from the 1970s will recognize the voice of David Gates. Clear, smooth and unaccented. Great melody as well.

Aquatones   **Say You'll Be Mine**   1958
> This is the second release by the group. Just as good as "You," though less well-known. Lynne Nixon's lead voice is clear and high.

Belairs   **Oh Baby**   1963
> New York group, New York style, with a song that borrows the "Ba-doo, ba-doo" riff from "Sincerely."

Carians   **She's Gone**   1961
> Excellent male version of the Chantels hit "He's Gone."

Chryslers, Little Nate &   **Someone Up There**   1959
This Nate is Nate Bouknight of the Shells. Overall sound of the Shells; dramatic, melodious and replete with falsetto running above and bass below Nate and his minions.

Classmates, Ronnie Jones &Lonely Boy   1958
Dramatic sound from this North Philly group. Lead Jones has a schoolboy voice.

Crescendos   **My Heart's Desire**   1960
Wanda Burt on lead for this Bay Area group. Two-sided hit, the flip being "Take My Heart."

Darts, Sherman & the   **Remember**   1957
Sherman Nichols is Sherman of the Darts. New York City dramatic ballad.

Del Rios   **Just Across The Street**   1962
Probably not the same Del Rios as on the rocker "Vines Of Love," but both groups have twang-laden leads.

Earls   **Without You**   1961
This group is known for their fast tunes, but they put out B-sides such as this one, "**Cross My Heart**" and "**All Through Our Teens**," which are similar, wonderful doo-wop ballads.

El Venos   **You Must Be True**   1957
This group was in hiding in Pittsburgh. They're great, with Anna Mae Jackson (aka Anne Keith) and Joey Daniels, alternating leads. We're in the tank for them, listing five of their songs in the Top 2000.

Enchanters   **I Lied To My Heart**   1961
New York City group. Good falsetto and bass.

Explorers   **I'm Simply Asking You**   1959
> Aka Dennis Lowell (aka Parnell) and the Explorers of "Vision of Love" fame. "**Don't Be A Fool**" was also added in the Top 2000.

Fabulous Pearl Devines   **So Lonely**   1959
> Latino group from Long Island, NY. Flip is "You've Been Gone," a fantastic uptempo on the first Top 1000.

King, Clyde & group   **Our Romance**   1957
> Young lady from California who's "trying to romance with you."

Majestics   **Sweet One**   1959
> White quintet from the Boston area.

Mon-Claires   **Please Come Back**   1962
> Sextet comprised of one female and five males. Strong melody, great mix of voices. From the Pittsburgh area.

Mystics   **Why Do You Pretend**   1958
> Actually by the Overons, the group that became the Mystics. This side is more "doo-woppy" than most Mystics sides, meaning more bass and falsetto and "doo-wah-wahs."

Serenaders   Never Let Me Go   1957
> Great group version of an original by Johnny Ace song from 1954. This group from Newark, NJ area provides a soulful rendition replete with soaring falsetto in the break.

How to Read and Use the Top 2000 Checklist

Each entry has a box and a circle next to it. The box can be checked if you "have" or own the track in question. The circle can be checked if you've heard the track. Or perhaps if the track is on your "want" or "need" list. If there are songs that the reader thinks should've been included, but weren't, the authors would like to hear from you.

Key: Entries in regular type are in the first 1000 songs
       Entries in **bold type** are from the **second 1000** songs

       FP= Fast tempo and Paleo-Doo-Wop
       MP= Medium tempo and Paleo-Doo-Wop
       SP= Slow tempo and Paleo-Doo-Wop
       FC= Fast tempo and Classical Doo-Wop
       MC= Medium tempo and Classical Doo-Wop
       SC= Slow tempo and Classical Doo-Wop
       FN= Fast tempo and Neo-Doo-Wop
       MN= Medium tempo and Neo-Doo-Wop
       SN= Slow tempo and Neo-Doo-Wop
       GG= (all-) girl group
       GL= girl lead, male group

Warning! This list is for the personal use and pleasure of authorized readers only. It may not be copied, distributed for profit or taken in vain; if you choose, however, it may be memorized at your own risk.

The Top 2000 Doo-Wop Songs

□○ Academics	Something Cool	1958	FC
□○ **Academics**	**Darla, My Darling**	**1956**	**FC**
□○ **Academics**	**Too Good To Be True**	**1957**	**FC**
□○ **Academics**	**Girl That I Love**	**1958**	**SC**
□○ **Accents (A)** **(Featuring Robert Draper Jr.)**	**Wiggle Wiggle**	**1958**	**FC**
□○ **Accents (B)** **David Gates & the**	**What's This I Hear**	**1960**	**SC**
□○ Adelphis	Kathleen	1958	FC
□○ Ad Libs	The Boy From New York City	1965	FN/ FL
□○ Admirations	The Bells Of Rosa Rita	1959	SC
□○ Admirations	It Happened So Fast	1961	SC
□○ **Affections,** **Judy & the**	**Dum, Dum, De Dip**	**1964**	**FC/ FG**
□○ Alaimo Quartet, The Chuck	How I Love You	1957	SC
□○ Alley Cats	Puddin' 'N 'Tain	1962	FN
□○ Ambassadors	Darling I'm Sorry	1954	SP
□○ Angels (A)	Wedding Bells Are Ringing In My Ears	1954	SP
□○ Angels (A)	Lovely Way To Spend An Evening	1954	SP
□○ Angels (B)	Til	1961	SN /FG

□○ **Angels (B)**	**A Moment Ago**	**1961**	**SN/ FG**
□○ **Angels (B)**	**Cry Baby Cry**	**1962**	**SN/ FG**
□○ **Angels (B)**	**Thank You And Goodnight**	**1963**	**SN/ FG**
□○ Angels (B)	My Boyfriend's Back	1963	FN /FG
□○ **Angels (C), Gabriel & the**	**Zing (Went The Strings Of My Heart)**	**1961**	**FN**
□○ **Antwinetts**	**Johnny**	**1958**	**FC/ FG**
□○ Aquatones	You	1958	SC /FG
□○ **Aquatones**	**Say You'll Be Mine**	**1958**	**SC/ FL**
□○ **Aquatones**	**Crazy For You**	**1960**	**SC/ FL**
□○ **Arcades**	**My Love**	**1959**	**SC**
□○ Arrogants	Mirror Mirror	1963	FN
□○ **Arrogants**	**Canadian Sunset**	**1963**	**FN**
□○ **Arrows, Joe Lyons & the**	**Shim Sham Shufflin' Jive**	**1959**	**FP**
□○ **Artistics**	**Life Begins At Sixteen**	**1962**	**SN**

□ ○ Astros, Pepe & the	Judy My Love (Judy Mi Amor)	1961	FN
□ ○ Audios, Cell Foster & the	I Prayed For You	1956	SC
□ ○ **Autumns**	**Dearest Little Angel**	**1962**	**FN**
□ ○ Avalons	My Heart's Desire	1958	SC
□ ○ **Avalons**	**You Can Count On Me**	**1959**	**FC**
□ ○ Avons	Our Love Will Never End	1956	FC
□ ○ Avons	Baby	1957	SC
□ ○ **Avons**	**Bonnie**	**1957**	**FC**
□ ○ Aztecs, Jose & the	My Aching Heart	1955	SC
□ ○ Bachelors (A) Dean Barlow & the)	Baby	1955	FC
□ ○ **Bachelors (B) (aka Jets)**	**You've Lied**	**1956**	**SP**
□ ○ Baltineers	Moments Like This	1956	SP
□ ○ Baltineers	Tears In My Eyes	1956	SP
□ ○ **Ban-Lons**	**Hey Baby**	**1962**	**FN**
□ ○ **Barons (A)**	**Eternally Yours**	**1955**	**SP**
□ ○ **Barons (B)**	**Pledge Of A Fool**	**1963**	**FN**
□ ○ **Barons (B)**	**Remember Rita**	**1964**	**FN**
□ ○ **Basin Street Boys**	**I Sold My Heart To The Junkman**	**1948**	**SP**

45

☐○ **Bay Bops**	**Follow The Rock**	**1958**	**FC**
☐○ **Bay Bops**	**Joanie**	**1958**	**FC**
☐○ **Beach Boys**	**Surfin'**	**1961**	**FN**
☐○ **Beach Boys**	**Surfer Girl**	**1963**	**SN**
☐○ **Bees**	**Sunny Side Of The Street**	**1954**	**FP**
☐○ **Bees**	**I Want To Be Loved**	**1954**	**SP**
☐○ **Bees**	**Toy Bell (My Ding-A-Ling)**	**1954**	**FP**
☐○ **Bel Aires**	**My Yearbook**	**1958**	**SC**
☐○ **Belairs**	**Oh Baby**	**1963**	**SC**
☐○ **Belangels**	**Ding Dong Bells**	**1995**	**FN**
☐○ **Belangels**	**That's The Way It Goes**	**1995**	**SC**
☐○ Bel-Larks	A Million And One Dreams	1963	SN
☐○ Bell Notes	I've Had It	1959	FC
☐○ **Belltones**	**Estelle**	**1954**	**SP**
☐○ **Belmonts**	**Tell Me Why**	**1961**	**FC**
☐○ **Belmonts**	**I Need Someone**	**1961**	**FN**
☐○ **Belmonts**	**Come On Little Angel**	**1962**	**FN**

☐○ Belmonts	Diddle De-Dum	1962	FN
☐○ Belmonts (Dion & the)	Don't Pity Me	1958	SC
☐○ Belmonts (Dion & the)	I Wonder Why	1958	FC
☐○ Belmonts (Dion & the)	No One Knows	1958	SC
☐○ Belmonts (Dion & the)	A Teenager In Love	1959	FC
☐○ Belmonts (Dion & the)	Where Or When	1960	SC
☐○ **Belmonts, Dion & the**	**That's My Desire**	**1960**	**SC**
☐○ **Belmonts, Dion & the**	**When You Wish Upon A Star**	**1960**	**SC**
☐○ **Belmonts, Dion & the**	**We Belong Together**	**1961**	**SN**
☐○ **Belmonts, Dion & the**	**I Wonder Why (live)**	**1972**	**FC**
☐○ Belvin, Jesse (& group)	Goodnight My Love	1956	SC
☐○ **Belvin, Jesse (& group)**	**Dear Heart**	**1956**	**SC**
☐○ **Belvin, Jesse (& group)**	**Endless Love**	**1959**	**SC**
☐○ **Berry Cups,**	**Hurt By A Letter**	**1959**	**SC**

47

Terry Clinton & the

□ ○ **Binders**	**You Don't Have To Cry Anymore**	**1970**	**SN**	
□ ○ Bing Bongs (Dicky Dell & the)	Ding-A-Ling A-Ling-Ding-Dong	1958	FC	
□ ○ Bishops	The Wedding	1961	SN	
□ ○ **Blades, Carol (with the Harptones)**	**When Will I know**	**1957**	**FC /FL**	
□ ○ Blenders	The Masquerade Is Over	1950	SP	
□ ○ Blenders	I'd Be A Fool Again	1952	SP	
□ ○ **Blenders**	**Don't Play (Fuck) Around With Love**	**1953**	**FP**	
□ ○ **Blossoms**	**Lonely Friday Night**	**1989**	**FC /FG**	
□ ○ **Blue Belles**	**I Sold My Heart To The Junkman**	**1962**	**FN/ FG**	
□ ○ Blue Belles (Patti LaBelle & the)	You'll Never Walk Alone	1963	SN /FG	
□ ○ Blue Jays	Let's Make Love	1961	SN	
□ ○ Blue Jays	Lover's Island	1961	SN	
□ ○ **Blue Jays, Leon Peels & the**	**Alice From Above**	**1989**	**SC**	
□ ○ **Blue Jays, Leon Peels & the**	**Once Upon A Love**	**1989**	**SC**	

□○ **Blue Jeans,** **Bobb B. Soxx & the**	**Zip-A-Dee Doo-Dah**	**1962**	**FN /FL**
□○ **Blue Jeans,** **Bobb B. Soxx & the**	**Not Too Young To Get** **Married**	**1963**	**FN /FL**
□○ Blue Jeans (Bobb B. Soxx & the)	Why Do Lovers Break Each Others Hearts	1963	FN /FL
□○ Blue Notes	If You Love Me	1956	SN
□○ Blue Notes	My Hero	1960	SN
□○ Blue Notes	Blue Star	1961	SN
□○ Bob Knight Four	Good Goodbye	1961	SC
□○ **Bob Knight Four**	**For Sale**	**1961**	**FN**
□○ **Bob-O-Links**	**I Promise**	**1962**	**SC**
□○ Bobbettes	Mr. Lee	1957	FC /FG
□○ Bonnevilles	Lorraine	1960	SC
□○ Bonnevilles	Zu Zu	1960	SC
□○ Bonnie Sisters	Cry Baby	1956	FC /FG
□○ Bop Chords	Castle In The Sky	1957	FC
□○ Bop Chords	I Really Love You	1957	SC
□○ Bop Chords	My Darling To You	1957	SC
□○ Bop Chords	So Why	1957	FC
□○ Bop Chords	When I Woke Up This Morning	1957	FC

☐○ **Bop Chords**	**My Darling To You**	**1957**	**SC**
☐○ Bosstones	Mope-itty Mope	1959	FN
☐○ **Boyfriends** (aka Five Discs)	**Let's Fall In Love**	**1964**	**FN**
☐○ Buccaneers	Dear Ruth	1953	SP
☐○ **Buccaneers**	**The Stars Will Remember**	**1953**	**SP**
☐○ **Buckeyes**	**Since I Fell For You**	**1957**	**SC**
☐○ C-Notes (aka C-Tones)	On Your Mark	1957	FC
☐○ **C-Notes (aka C-Tones**	**Forever And Ever**	**1961**	**SC**
☐○ **C-Notes (aka C-Tones**	**Last Saturday Night**	**1959**	**SC**
☐○ Cabineers	Each Time	1951	SP
☐○ Cadets	Fools Rush In	1956	FC
☐○ Cadets	Stranded In The Jungle	1956	FC
☐○ **Cadets**	**Church Bells May Ring**	**1956**	**FC**
☐○ **Cadets**	**Ring Chimes**	**1957**	**FC**
☐○ Cadillacs	Gloria	1954	SP
☐○ Cadillacs	I Wonder Why	1954	SP
☐○ Cadillacs	Wishing Well	1954	SP
☐○ **Cadillacs**	**Party For Two**	**1954**	**FC**

□○ Cadillacs	Down The Road	1955	FP
□○ Cadillacs	Speedoo	1955	FP
□○ Cadillacs	Sympathy	1955	SP
□○ **Cadillacs**	**No Chance**	**1955**	**FC**
□○ **Cadillacs**	**Window Lady**	**1955**	**SC**
□○ Cadillacs	The Girl I Love	1956	FP
□○ Cadillacs	You Are	1956	SP
□○ Cadillacs	Zoom	1956	FP
□○ **Cadillacs**	**Betty My Love**	**1956**	**SC**
□○ **Cadillacs**	**Woe Is Me**	**1956**	**FC**
□○ Cadillacs	My Girl Friend	1957	FP
□○ **Cadillacs**	**Peek A Boo**	**1958**	**FC**
□○ **Calvaes**	**Fine Girl**	**1956**	**FC**
□○ **Calvanes**	**Crazy Over You**	**1955**	**FP**
□○ **Calvanes**	**Fleeoowee**	**1972**	**FP**
□○ Calvanes	Don't Take Your Love From Me	1955	SC
□○ Camelots (aka Cupids/Harps)	Don't Leave Me Baby	1964	FC
□○ **Cameos**	**Wait Up**	**1960**	**FN**
□○ **Camerons**	**Cheryl**	**1960**	**FN**

51

□○ **Camerons**	**Guardian Angel**	**1961**	**FN**
□○ Candles, Rochell & the	Once Upon A Time	1960	SN
□○ **Candles, Rochell & the**	**Long Time Ago**	**1961**	**SN**
□○ Candles, Rochell & the	Each Night	1962	SN
□○ Cap-Tans	I'm So Crazy For Love	1950	SP
□○ Cap-Tans	With All My Love	1950	SP
□○ **Cap-Tans**	**Crazy 'Bout My Honey Dip**	**1950**	**FP**
□○ Capistranos (John Littleton & the)	Now Darling	1958	SC
□○ **Capitols**	**Angel Of Love**	**1958**	**SC**
□○ **Capitols, Mickey Toliver & the**	**Rose-Marie**	**1957**	**FC**
□○ **Capitols, Mickey Toliver & the**	**Day By Day**	**1958**	**FC /FL**
□○ Capris (A)	God Only Knows	1954	SP /FL
□○ Capris (A)	It Was Moonglow	1954	SP /FL
□○ **Capris (A)**	**That's What You're Doing To Me**	**1954**	**FC/ FL**
□○ **Capris (A)**	**Oh My Darling**	**1958**	**SC/ FL**

□○ Capris (B)	There's A Moon Out Tonight	1958	SN
□○ **Capris (B)**	**Darling**	**1958**	**SC**
□○ Capris (B)	Where I Fell In Love	1961	SN
□○ **Capris (B)**	**Guardian Angel**	**1982**	**FC**
□○ **Capris (B)**	**That's How Love Goes**	**1982**	**SN**
□○ Capris (B)	Morse Code Of Love	1982	FN
□○ Cardinals	Shouldn't I Know	1951	SP
□○ Cardinals	Wheel Of Fortune	1952	SP
□○ Cardinals	You Are My Only Love	1953	SP
□○ Cardinals	Under A Blanket Of Blue	1954	SP
□○ Cardinals	The Door Is Still Open	1955	SP
□○ **Cardinals**	**Come Back My Love**	**1955**	**FP**
□○ Cardinals	Off Shore	1956	SP
□○ **Carians**	**She's Gone**	**1961**	**SC**
□○ Carnations (aka Startones)	Long Tall Girl	1961	FC
□○ Carollons (Lonnie & the)	Chapel Of Tears	1960	SN
□○ Carousels	You Can Come (If You Want To)	1961	SN /FG
□○ **Casanovas**	**That's All**	**1955**	**SC**

□ ○ **Casinos**	**Then You Can Tell Me Goodbye**	**1962**	**SN**
□ ○ Caslons	Anniversary Of Love	1961	FN
□ ○ **Castaleers**	**I'll Be Around**	**1959**	**SC**
□ ○ Castelles	My Girls Awaits Me	1953	SP
□ ○ **Castelles**	**Marcella**	**1954**	**SP**
□ ○ Castelles	Do You Remember	1954	SP
□ ○ Castelles	Over A Cup Of Coffee	1954	SP
□ ○ Castelles	This Silver Ring	1954	SP
□ ○ Castelles	Heavenly Father	1955	SP
□ ○ **Castells**	**Sacred**	**1961**	**SN**
□ ○ Castells	So This Is Love	1962	SN
□ ○ **Castle-Tones**	**We Met At A Dance**	**1960**	**SC**
□ ○ Castro, Vince (w/ the Tonettes)	Bong Bong (I Love You Madly)	1958	FC
□ ○ Castroes	Dearest Darling	1959	SC
□ ○ **Casuals**	**So Tough**	**1958**	**FC**
□ ○ **Catalina 6**	**Would You Believe It**	**1962**	**SN**
□ ○ **Cates, Ronnie (bb/Travelers)**	**For My Very Own**	**1962**	**FN**
□ ○ Cavaliers	Dance Dance Dance	1958	FC
□ ○ Cavaliers	The Magic Age Of Sixteen	1963	SN

□○ Cellos	Rang Tang Ding Dong (I Am the Japanese Sandman)	1957	FC
□○ Cellos	You Took My Love	1957	SC
□○ **Cellos**	**Girlie That I Love**	**1957**	**FC**
□○ Chalets	Fat Fat Mommio	1961	FC
□○ **Champs, Tony Allen & the**	**Nite Owl**	**1955**	**FP**
□○ **Chancellors**	**There Goes My Girl**	**1957**	**FC**
□○ Chandeliers (aka Chandeliers Quintet)	Blueberry Sweet	1958	FC
□○ **Chandeliers (aka Chandeliers Quintet)**	**Dancing In The Congo**	**1958**	**FC**
□○ Chandler, Gene (w/Dukays)	Duke Of Earl	1961	MN
□○ Channels, Earl Lewis & the	Now You Know (I Love You So)	1956	FC
□○ Channels, Earl Lewis & the	The Closer You Are	1956	SC
□○ Channels, Earl Lewis & the	The Gleam In Your Eyes	1956	SC
□○ **Channels, Earl Lewis & the**	**Stars In The Sky**	**1956**	**FC**
□○ **Channels, Earl Lewis & the**	**I Really Love You**	**1956**	**SC**

☐○ **Channels, Earl Lewis & the**	**Gloria**	**1956**	**SC**
☐○ Channels, Earl Lewis & the	Bye Bye Baby	1957	FC
☐○ Channels, Earl Lewis & the	Flames In My Heart	1957	SC
☐○ Channels, Earl Lewis & the	My Love Will Never Die	1957	SC
☐○ Channels, Earl Lewis & the	That's My Desire	1957	SC
☐○ **Channels, Earl Lewis & the**	**Altar Of Love**	**1958**	**SC**
☐○ **Channels, Earl Lewis & the**	**The Girl Next Door**	**1959**	**SC**
☐○ **Channels, Earl Lewis & the**	**Do What Lovers Do**	**1989**	**FC**
☐○ Chantels	He's Gone	1957	SC /FG
☐○ **Chantels**	**The Plea**	**1957**	**SC /FG**
☐○ **Chantels**	**Every Night (I Pray)**	**1958**	**SC /FG**
☐○ Chantels	Maybe	1958	SC /FG
☐○ **Chantels**	**I Love You So**	**1958**	**SC /FG**

□○ **Chantels**	**Prayee**	**1958**	**SC /FG**
□○ **Chantels**	**Goodbye To Love**	**1959**	**SC /FG**
□○ Chantels	Look In My Eyes	1961	SC /FG
□○ Chanters	Angel Darling	1958	SC
□○ Chanters	I Need Your Tenderness	1958	SC
□○ Chanters	My My Darling	1958	FC
□○ Chanters	No No No	1958	FC
□○ **Chanters**	**Stars In The Sky**	**1958**	**FC**
□○ **Chanters**	**Five Little Kisses**	**1958**	**FC**
□○ **Chanters**	**At My Door**	**1961**	**FC**
□○ **Chanters**	**Row Your Boat**	**1963**	**FC**
□○ Chaperones	Cruise To The Moon	1960	SN
□○ Charades	Please Be My Love Tonight	1963	SN
□○ **Chargers (w/Jesse Belvin)**	**Old McDonald**	**1958**	**FC**
□○ Chariots	Gloria	1959	SC
□○ Charles, Jimmy (w/Revelettes)	A Million To One	1960	SN
□○ **Charmers**	**Tony, My Darling**	**1954**	**SP/ FL**

57

□ ○ **Charmers**	**The Beating Of My Heart**	**1954**	**SP/ FL**
□ ○ **Charmettes**	**Please Don't Kiss Me Again**	**1963**	**FN/ FG**
□ ○ Charms, Otis Williams & the	Ivory Tower	1954	SC
□ ○ Charms, Otis Williams & the	My Baby Dearest Darling	1954	FC
□ ○ Charms, Otis Williams & the	Two Hearts	1954	FC
□ ○ **Charms, Otis Williams & the**	**Hearts Of Stone**	**1954**	**FC**
□ ○ Charms, Otis Williams & the	Gumdrop	1956	FC
□ ○ Charms, Otis Williams & the	One Night Only	1956	FC
□ ○ **Charms, Otis Williams & the**	**I'd Like To Thank You Mr. D.J.**	**1956**	**SC**
□ ○ **Charters**	**Lost In A Dream**	**1963**	**SC**
□ ○ Charts	Dance Girl	1957	FC
□ ○ Charts	Desiree	1957	SC
□ ○ Charts	Why Do You Cry	1957	SC
□ ○ Charts	You're The Reason	1957	SC
□ ○ Charts	Zoop	1957	FC
□ ○ **Charts**	**My Diane**	**1957**	**SC**

□○ **Chavelles**	**Valley Of Love**	**1956**	**SC**
□○ Checkers	Nights Curtains	1952	SP
□○ Checkers	Ghost Of My Baby	1953	SP
□○ **Checkers**	**My Prayer Tonight**	**1953**	**SP**
□○ **Checkers**	**House With No Windows**	**1954**	**SP**
□○ **Checkers**	**Over The Rainbow**	**1954**	**FP**
□○ Checkers	White Cliffs Of Dover	1954	FP
□○ **Cherokees (A)**	**Rainbow Of Love**	**1954**	**SP**
□○ **Cherokees (A)**	**Please Tell Me So**	**1954**	**SP**
□○ Cherokees (B)	My Heavenly Angel	1961	FN
□○ **Chessman**	**Ways Of Romance**	**1965**	**FN**
□○ **Chessmen**	**Heavenly Father**	**1965**	**SN**
□○ **Chessmen**	**All Nite Long**	**1965**	**FN**
□○ Chesters	The Fires Burn No More	1958	SC
□○ Chestnuts	Love Is True	1956	SC /FL
□○ **Chestnuts**	**Forever I Vow**	**1956**	**SC/ FL**
□○ Chevrons	Lullabye	1959	FC
□○ Chex, Tex & the	I Do Love You	1961	SN

59

□○ **Chic Chocs**	**Them There Eyes**	**1961**	**FN/ FG**
□○ Chiffons	He's So Fine	1963	FN /FG
□○ Chiffons	I Have A Boyfriend	1963	FN /FG
□○ Chiffons	Oh My Lover	1963	FN /FG
□○ Chiffons	One Fine Day	1963	FN /FG
□○ **Chiffons**	**A Love So Fine**	**1963**	**FN/ FG**
□○ **Chiffons**	**Tonight I Met An Angel**	**1963**	**FN/ FG**
□○ **Chiffons**	**I Wonder Why**	**1963**	**FC /FG**
□○ **Chimes (A)**	**The Chimes (The Chimes Ring Out)**	**1955**	**SC**
□○ Chimes (B)	Once In A While	1960	SN
□○ **Chimes (B)**	**Dream Girl**	**1961**	**FC**
□○ **Chimes (B)**	**Let's Fall In Love**	**1961**	**SN**
□○ Chimes (B)	I'm In The Mood For Love	1961	SN
□○ Chips	Oh, My Darlin'	1956	SC
□○ Chips (A)	Rubber Biscuit	1956	FC

□○ **Chips (B)**	**Darling (I Need Your Love)**	**1960**	**MC**
□○ **Choice**	**Everyone's Laughing**	**1996**	**MC**
□○ **Choice**	**Great Jumpin' Catfish**	**1996**	**FC**
□○ **Choice**	**In My Lonely Room**	**1996**	**SC**
□○ **Choice**	**Peace Of Mind**	**1996**	**SC**
□○ **Choice**	**Two Loves Have I**	**1996**	**SC**
□○ **Chordettes**	**Lollypop**	**1954**	**FC**
□○ Chords	Sh-Boom	1954	FP
□○ **Chords**	**Bless You (For Being An Angel)**	**1954**	**SP**
□○ **Chryslers, Little Nate & the**	**Someone Up There**	**1959**	**SC**
□○ **Chuck-A-Lucks**	**Heaven Knows (I Love You)**	**1957**	**SC**
□○ **Church, Eugene & group**	**Open Up Your Heart**	**1957**	**SC**
□○ **Cineramas**	**Life Can Be Beautiful**	**1958**	**SC**
□○ **Citadels**	**When I Woke Up This Morning**	**1965**	**FN**
□○ **Claremonts**	**Angel Of Romance**	**1957**	**SC/ FG**

□○ Clark, Dee (bb the Kool Gents)	Just Like A Fool	1960	SC
□○ Classic IV	Island Of Paradise	1962	SN
□○ **Classics**	**Cinderella**	**1959**	**FN**
□○ **Classics**	**So In Love**	**1959**	**SC**
□○ Classics	Till Then	1963	SN
□○ **Classmates, Ronnie Jones & the**	**Little Girl Next Door**	**1957**	**SC**
□○ **Classmates, Ronnie Jones & the**	**Lonely Boy**	**1958**	**SC**
□○ **Clefftones**	**Gloria**	**1955**	**SC**
□○ **Clefftones**	**Little Girl (I Love You Madly)**	**1955**	**FC**
□○ **Clefftones**	**My Dearest Darling**	**1955**	**SC**
□○ Clefs	We Three	1952	SP
□○ Cleftones	Can't We Be Sweethearts?	1956	FC
□○ Cleftones	Little Girl Of Mine	1956	FC
□○ Cleftones	String Around My Heart	1956	FC
□○ Cleftones	You Baby You	1956	FC
□○ **Cleftones**	**You're Driving Me Mad**	**1956**	**SC**
□○ **Cleftones**	**Happy Memories**	**1956**	**FC**
□○ Cleftones	See You Next Year	1957	SC

□○ Cleftones	Why You Do Me Like You Do	1957	FC
□○ **Cleftones**	**Lover Boy**	**1958**	**FC**
□○ **Cleftones**	**She's So Fine**	**1958**	**FC**
□○ **Cleftones**	**I Love You For Sentimental Reasons**	**1961**	**FC**
□○ Cleftones	Heart And Soul	1961	MN
□○ **Cleftones (w/Pat Spann)**	**Heavenly Father**	**1961**	**SC /FL**
□○ **Cleftones (w/Pat Spann)**	**Please Say You Want Me**	**1961**	**SC /FL**
□○ **Cleftones, Herb Cox & the**	**My Angel Lover**	**1989**	**FC**
□○ **Cleftones, Herb Cox & the**	**You Lost The Game Of Love**	**1989**	**SC**
□○ Click-Ettes	Lover's Prayer	1960	SN /FG
□○ **Clickettes**	**But Not For Me**	**1960**	**SN/ FG**
□○ **Clickettes, Barbara English & the**	**I Love You, I Swear**	**2013**	**SN/ FG**
□○ **Cliftones**	**School Is Over**	**1976**	**FC**
□○ **Clippers, Johnny Blake & the**	**Bella Marie**	**1957**	**FC**

63

☐○ Cliques	Girl In My Dreams	1956	SC
☐○ Clovermen, Tippie & the	**Please Mr. Sun**	**1962**	**SC**
☐○ Clovers	Yes Sir, That's My Baby	1950	SP
☐○ Clovers	Fool, Fool, Fool	1951	FP
☐○ Clovers	Needless	1951	SP
☐○ Clovers	Skylark	1951	SP
☐○ Clovers	I Played The Fool	1952	SP
☐○ Clovers	One Mint Julep	1952	FP
☐○ Clovers	**Ting-A-Ling**	**1952**	**FP**
☐○ Clovers	**Good Lovin'**	**1953**	**FP**
☐○ Clovers	**Lovey Dovey**	**1954**	**FP**
☐○ Clovers	**Your Cash Ain't Nothin' But Trash**	**1954**	**FP**
☐○ Clovers	**Nip Sip**	**1955**	**FP**
☐○ Clovers	Blue Velvet	1955	SP
☐○ Clovers	Devil Or Angel	1956	SP
☐○ Clovers	Love Potion No. 9	1959	FC
☐○ Clusters	Darling Can't You Tell	1958	FC
☐○ Clusters	**Pardon My Heart**	**1958**	**SC**
☐○ Co-Eds, Gwen Edwards & the	**Love You Baby All The Time**	**1956**	**FC/ FL**

□○ **Co-Eds, Gwen Edwards & the**	**I'm In Love**	**1957**	**FC/ FL**
□○ Coasters	Down In Mexico	1956	FC
□○ **Coasters**	**Brazil**	**1956**	**FP**
□○ Coasters	Searchin'	1957	MC
□○ Coasters	Young Blood	1957	FC
□○ **Coasters**	**Zing Went The Strings Of My Heart**	**1958**	**FC**
□○ Coasters	Yakety Yak	1958	FC
□○ Coasters	Along Came Jones	1959	FC
□○ Coasters	Charlie Brown	1959	FC
□○ Coasters	Poison Ivy	1959	FC
□○ **Coasters**	**Little Egypt**	**1961**	**FC**
□○ Cobras	La La	1964	FN
□○ Coins	Blue, Can't Get No Place With You	1954	FC
□○ Collegians	Zoom Zoom Zoom	1957	FC
□○ **Collegians**	**On Your Merry Way**	**1957**	**SC**
□○ Collegians	Heavenly Night	1958	SC
□○ Collegians	Let's Go For A Ride	1958	FC
□○ **Colonairs**	**Sandy**	**1957**	**FC**

65

□ ○ Colts	Adorable	1955	FC
□ ○ Columbus Pharaohs	Give Me Your Love	1957	SC
□ ○ **Columbus Pharaohs**	**China Girl**	**1958**	**FC**
□ ○ **Computones**	**Flip Flip Zu-Wah**	**1965**	**FN**
□ ○ **Computones**	**Dottie**	**1965**	**FN**
□ ○ **Concepts**	**Yo Me Pregunto**	**1966**	**FN**
□ ○ **Concepts**	**Jungle**	**1961**	**FN**
□ ○ Concords	Candlelight	1954	SP
□ ○ **Concords**	**Again**	**1961**	**FN**
□ ○ **Concords**	**Cross My Heart**	**1961**	**FN**
□ ○ **Confidential Four**	**Walking On A Cloud**	**1964**	**SC**
□ ○ **Confidential Four**	**Please Be My Girlfriend**	**1966**	**FN**
□ ○ **Connotations**	**Before I Go**	**1962**	**SC**
□ ○ **Consoles, Bobby & the**	**My Jelly Bean**	**1963**	**FN**
□ ○ Consorts	Please Be Mine	1961	FN
□ ○ Contenders	The Clock	1963	FN
□ ○ **Contenders**	**Hetta Hetta**	**1966**	**FN**

□○ **Continental Five**	**My Lonely Friend**	**1959**	**FC**
□○ Continentals (A)	Dear Lord	1956	SC
□○ Continentals (A)	Fine Fine Frame	1956	FC
□○ Continentals (A)	Picture Of Love	1956	FC
□○ Continentals (A)	Soft And Sweet	1956	SC
□○ Continentals (A)	You're An Angel	1956	SC
□○ **Continentals (B) and the Counts Of Rhythm**	**Don't Leave Me**	**1958**	**FC**
□○ **Continentals (C), Teddy & the**	**Tick Tick Tock**	**1961**	**FC**
□○ Convincers	Rejected Love	1962	SN
□○ **Cookies (A)**	**In Paradise**	**1956**	**FC /FG**
□○ Cookies (B)	Chains	1962	FN /FG
□○ Cookies (B)	Don't Say Nothin' Bad (About My Baby	1963	FN /FG
□○ **Coolbreezers**	**The Greatest Love Of All**	**1958**	**SC**
□○ Copasetics	Collegian	1956	FC /FL
□○ **Cordell, Ritchie & group**	**Tick Tock**	**1962**	**FN**
□○ Cordells	The Beat Of My Heart	1961	FN

67

□○ **Cordials**	**Dawn Is Almost Here**	**1962**	**SN**
□○ Cordovans	Come On Baby	1960	FC
□○ Coronets	Nadine	1953	SP
□○ Corsairs	Smoky Places	1961	MN
□○ Corvairs	True True Love	1962	FN
□○ **Corvells**	**The Bells**	**1961**	**FN**
□○ **Corvells**	**Take My Love**	**1962**	**FN**
□○ Cosmic Rays	Daddy's Gonna Tell You No Lies	1960	FC
□○ **Counts**	**My Dear, My Darling**	**1954**	**SC**
□○ **Court Jesters**	**Roaches**	**1961**	**FN**
□○ Creations	Woke Up In The Morning	1961	FC
□○ **Crescendos (A)**	**Ding A Ling**	**1956**	**FC**
□○ Crescendos (B)	Oh Julie	1957	SC
□○ **Crescendos (C)**	**My Heart's Desire**	**1960**	**SC/ FL**
□○ **Crescendos (C)**	**Take My Heart**	**1960**	**SC/ FL**
□○ Crescents (A), Pat Cordel & the	Darling Come Back	1956	FC /FL
□○ Crescents (B)	Everybody Knew But Me	1957	SC
□○ **Crestones, Jimmy & the**	**Angel Maureen**	**1964**	**SN**

☐○ Crests	My Juanita	1957	FC
☐○ Crests	No One To Love	1957	SC
☐○ Crests	Sweetest One	1957	SC
☐○ Crests	Sixteen Candles	1958	SC
☐○ **Crests**	**Pretty Little Angel**	**1958**	**FC**
☐○ **Crests**	**Six Nights A Week**	**1959**	**SC**
☐○ **Crests**	**A Year Ago Tonight**	**1959**	**SC**
☐○ Crests	The Angels Listened In	1959	FC
☐○ Crests	Isn't It Amazing	1960	FC
☐○ Crests	Step By Step	1960	FC
☐○ Crests	Trouble In Paradise	1960	FC
☐○ **Crests**	**Guilty**	**1962**	**SC**
☐○ Crickets, Dean Barlow & the	You're Mine	1953	SP
☐○ **Crickets, Dean Barlow & the**	**Be Faithful**	**1953**	**SP**
☐○ Crickets, Dean Barlow & the	Your Love	1954	SP
☐○ **Crisis, Lonnie & the**	**Bells In The Chapel**	**1961**	**SN**
☐○ **Criterions**	**Don't Say Goodbye**	**1959**	**SC**

□○ Crowns, Arthur   I Wanna Love   1954   FC
      Lee Maye & the

□○ Crowns, (Arthur   Love Me Always   1955   SC
      Lee Maye & the

□○ Crowns, Arthur   Truly   1955   SC
      Lee Maye & the

□○ **Crowns, Arthur   Cool Lovin'   1955   FC**
      Lee Maye & the

□○ **Crowns, Arthur   Please Don't Leave Me   1955   SC**
      Lee Maye & the

□○ **Crowns, Arthur   Oh-Rooba-Lee   1956   FC**
      Lee Maye & the

□○ Crowns, Arthur   Gloria   1956   SC
      Lee Maye & the

□○ Crowns, Arthur   This Is The Night For Love   1956   SC
      Lee Maye & the

□○ **Crowns, Arthur   Hey Pretty Girl   1957   FC**
      Lee Maye & the

□○ **Crowns, Arthur   I'll Have Memories Of You 1957   SC**
      Lee Maye & the

□○ **Crowns, Arthur   Honey Honey   1958   FC**
      Lee Maye & the

□○ **Crowns, Arthur   All I Want Is Someone   1958   SC**
      Lee Maye & the   To Love

□○ **Crowns, Arthur   Don't You Know (I Love   1985   FC**
      Lee Maye & the   You So

☐○ **Crows (w/Viola Watkins)**	**Seven Lonely Days**	**1953**	**SP**
☐○ Crows	Gee	1954	FP
☐○ Crows	I Love You So	1954	SP
☐○ Crows	Miss You	1954	SP
☐○ Crows	Untrue	1954	SP
☐○ **Crows**	**Heartbreaker**	**1954**	**SC**
☐○ Crows	Baby Doll	1955	FC
☐○ **Cruisers**	**If I Knew**	**1960**	**SC**
☐○ **Cruisers**	**Crying Over You**	**1960**	**SN**
☐○ **Crystalairs**	**Ding Dong Teenage Bells**	**1991**	**FN**
☐○ **Crystalairs**	**Frag' Nicht Warum (I Wonder Why)**	**1991**	**FN**
☐○ **Crystaliers, Cleo & the**	**Please Be My Guy**	**1957**	**FC/ FL**
☐○ Crystals	There's No Other (Like My Baby)	1961	SN /FG
☐○ Crystals	He's Sure The Boy I Love	1962	FN /FG
☐○ **Crystals**	**He's A Rebel**	**1962**	**FN/ FG**
☐○ **Crystals**	**Then He Kissed Me**	**1963**	**FN/ FG**

71

□○ Crystals	Da Doo Ron Ron	1963	FN /FG
□○ **Cubs**	**I Hear Wedding Bells**	**1956**	**SC**
□○ Cuff Links	Guided Missiles	1957	SC
□○ **Cuff Links**	**It's Too Late Now**	**1957**	**SC**
□○ **Cuff Links**	**So Tough**	**1958**	**FC**
□○ **Cupids (A)**	**Troubles Not At End**	**1956**	**SC**
□○ Cupids (B)	Brenda	1962	SN
□○ **Cupids (B)**	**(If You Cry) True Love True Love**	**1962**	**FN**
□○ **Curtiss, Jimmy (bb/Regents)**	**Let's Dance Close**	**1965**	**SN**
□○ **Dahills**	**She's My Angel**	**1978**	**FN**
□○ Danderliers	My Autumn Love	1955	SC
□○ **Danderliers**	**Chop Chop Boom**	**1955**	**FC**
□○ **Danderliers**	**May God Be With You**	**1956**	**SC**
□○ Danleers	One Summer Night	1958	SC
□○ Danleers	I Really Love You	1958	SC
□○ **Danleers**	**Picture Of You**	**1958**	**FC**
□○ **Dappers**	**Come Back To Me**	**1955**	**SP**

□○ **Darchaes, Ray & the**	**When I Woke Up This Morning**	**1961**	**FC**
□○ **Darchaes, Ray & the**	**Little Girl So Fine**	**1962**	**FC**
□○ Darchaes, Ray & the	Carol	1962	SN
□○ **Darchaes, Ben White & the**	**Jocko Sent Me**	**1962**	**SC**
□○ **Darchaes, Nicky Addeo & the**	**Gloria**	**1963**	**SC**
□○ **Darts, Sherman & the**	**Remember (It's Only You And I)**	**1957**	**SC**
□○ **Darvells, Frankie & the**	**Mr. Fortune Teller**	**1977**	**FN**
□○ **Dates, Lincoln Fig & the**	**Way Up**	**1958**	**FC**
□○ **Day, Bobby (w/Satellites)**	**Rockin' Robin**	**1958**	**FC**
□○ **Day, Darlene (bb/Imaginations)**	**I Love You So**	**1961**	**SC/ FL**
□○ **Daychords, Roxy & the**	**I'm So In Love**	**1962**	**SN/ FL**
□○ **De Vaurs**	**Teenager**	**1958**	**FC/ FG**
□○ Debonaires	Darling	1957	FC

□○ **Debonaires**	**Every Once In A While**	**1959**	**SC**
□○ **Debonairs** (aka Debonaires)	**Cause Of A Bad Romance**	**1958**	**SC**
□○ Decoys	It's Gonna Be Allright	1963	FN
□○ **Decoys**	**I Only Want You**	**1963**	**SN/ FL**
□○ **Decoys**	**Memories**	**1963**	**SN/ FL**
□○ **Decoys**	**Tomorrow**	**1964**	**FN/ FL**
□○ **Del Chateaus**	**Sunday Kind Of Love**	**1964**	**FN**
□○ **Del Larks, Sammy & the**	**Remember The Night**	**1958**	**FC**
□○ **Del-Chords**	**Say That You Love Me**	**1960**	**FC**
□○ **Del Rays**	**Around The Corner**	**1959**	**FC**
□○ **Del Rios**	**Vines Of Love**	**1958**	**FC**
□○ **Del Rios**	**Just Across The Street**	**1958**	**SN**
□○ **Del Satins**	**Remember**	**1961**	**FN**
□○ **Del Satins**	**I'll Pray For You**	**1961**	**SN**
□○ Del Satins	Teardrops Follow Me	1962	FN
□○ **Del Shays**	**(Love You) Forever**	**1964**	**FN**
□○ **Delacardos**	**Letter To A Schoolgirl**	**1959**	**SC**

□○ Delighters (Donald Jenkins & the)	(Native Girl) Elephant Walk	1963	FN
□○ **Dellchords, David Campanella & the**	**Somewhere Over The Rainbow**	**1959**	**SC**
□○ **Dellchords, David Campanella & the**	**Everything's That Way**	**1959**	**FC**
□○ Dell Vikings	A Sunday Kind Of Love	1957	FC
□○ Dell Vikings	Come Go With Me	1957	FC
□○ Dell Vikings	I'm Spinning	1957	FC
□○ Dell Vikings	When I Come Home	1957	SC
□○ Dell Vikings	Whispering Bells	1957	FC
□○ **Dell Vikings**	**Somewhere Over The Rainbow**	**1957**	**SC**
□○ **Dell Vikings**	**How Can I Find True Love**	**1957**	**SC**
□○ **Dells**	**Dreams Of Contentment**	**1955**	**SC**
□○ **Dells**	**Zing Zing Zing**	**1955**	**FC**
□○ Dells	Tell The World	1955	SC
□○ Dells	Oh What A Night	1956	SC
□○ Dells	Time Makes You Change	1957	FC
□○ Dells	Why Do You Have To Go	1957	SC
□○ Dells	Dry Your Eyes	1959	SC
□○ Delmonicos	World's Biggest Fool	1964	SN

□○ **Delmonicos**	**Cynthia**	**1958**	**SC**
□○ Delrons, Reperata & the	Whenever A Teenager Cries	1964	SN /FG
□○ Delrons, Reperata & the	Tommy	1965	SN /FG
□○ Delroys	Bermuda Shorts	1957	FC
□○ Deltairs	Lullabye Of The Bells	1957	SC /FG
□○ Deltas	Lamplight	1957	FC
□○ Demens	Take Me As I Am	1957	SC
□○ Demensions	Over The Rainbow	1962	SN
□○ **Demensions**	**Just One More Chance**	**1963**	**FN**
□○ **Demensions**	**My Foolish Heart**	**1963**	**SN**
□○ Demilles	Donna Lee	1964	FN
□○ **Demons, Eddie Jones & the**	**The Greatest Of Them All**	**1957**	**SC**
□○ Desires	Hey, Lena	1959	FC
□○ Desires	Let It Please Be You	1959	SC
□○ Desires	I Wanna Rendezvous With You	1960	FC
□○ **Desires**	**Set Me Free (My Darling)**	**1960**	**SC**
□○ Devotions	Rip Van Winkle	1961	FN

□○ **Devotions**	**(I Love You) For Sentimental Reasons**	**1961**	**SC**
□○ **Devotions**	**Sunday Kind Of Love**	**1964**	**FN**
□○ Diablos	The Wind	1954	SP
□○ Diablos, Nolan Strong & the	Adios My Desert Love	1954	SC
□○ Diablos, Nolan Strong & the	Hold Me Until Eternity	1955	SC
□○ **Diablos, Nolan Strong & the**	**The Way You Dog Me Around**	**1955**	**SC**
□○ Diablos, Nolan Strong & the	Can't We Talk This Over	1957	SC
□○ Diablos, Nolan Strong & the	If I (Could Be With You Tonight)	1959	FC
□○ **Diablos, Nolan Strong & the**	**I Wanna Know**	**1959**	**SC**
□○ Diablos, Nolan Strong & the	Since You're Gone	1960	SC
□○ **Diablos, Nolan Strong & the**	**Mind Over Matter**	**1962**	**FN**
□○ **Diablos, Nolan Strong & the**	**Someday You'll Want Me To Want You**	**1984**	**SC**
□○ **Diablos, Nolan Strong & the**	**Since I Fell For You**	**1984**	**SC**
□○ **Dials (A)**	**School Bells Are Ringing**	**1961**	**SN**

77

□○ **Dials (B)**	**At The Start Of A New Romance**	**1962**	**FN**
□○ Dialtones	Til I Heard It From You	1960	FN /FL
□○ Diamonds (A)	A Beggar For Your Kisses	1952	SP
□○ Diamonds (A)	Cherry	1953	SP
□○ Diamonds (A)	Two Loves Have I	1953	SP
□○ **Diamonds (B)**	**Little Darlin'**	**1957**	**FC**
□○ **Diddley, Bo & group**	**I'm Sorry**	**1959**	**SC**
□○ **Dillard, Varetta & the Four Students**	**Darling Listen To The Words Of This Song**	**1956**	**SC**
□○ **DiMucci, Dion & group**	**Lonely Teenager**	**1960**	**FN**
□○ DiMucci, Dion (w/Del Satins)	Runaround Sue	1961	FN
□○ **DiMucci, Dion (w/Del Satins)**	**The Wanderer**	**1961**	**FN**
□○ DiMucci, Dion (w/Del Satins)	Lovers Who Wander	1962	FN
□○ **DiMucci, Dion (w/Del Satins)**	**Love Came To Me**	**1962**	**FN**
□○ DiMucci, Dion (w/Del Satins)	Donna The Prima Donna	1963	FN

□○ **DiMucci, Dion** (w/Del Satins)	**Ruby Baby**	**1963**	**FN**
□○ **DiMucci, Dion** (w/Del Satins)	**Drip Drop**	**1963**	**FN**
□○ **DiMucci, Dion** (w/Del Satins)	**Sandy**	**1963**	**FN**
□○ Diplomats, Dino & the	Hushabye My Love	1961	FN
□○ Diplomats, Dino & the	I Can't Believe	1961	FN
□○ **Diplomats, Dino & the**	**My Dream**	**1961**	**FN**
□○ Dodgers	Drip Drop	1955	SP
□○ **Domineers**	**Nothing Can Go Wrong**	**1960**	**FC**
□○ Dominoes	Do Something For Me	1950	SP
□○ Dominoes	Harbor Lights	1951	SP
□○ Dominoes	Sixty Minute Man	1951	FP
□○ **Dominoes**	**That's What You're Doing To Me**	**1951**	**FP**
□○ Dominoes	Have Mercy Baby	1952	FP
□○ Dominoes	I'd Be Satisfied	1952	SP
□○ Dominoes	The Bells	1952	SP
□○ Dominoes	When The Swallows Come Back To Capistrano	1952	SP

□ ○ Dominoes	These Foolish Things	1953	SP
□ ○ **Dominoes**	**I'm Gonna Move To The Outskirts Of Town**	**1954**	**SP**
□ ○ Dominoes	Deep Purple	1957	SP
□ ○ Dominoes	Stardust	1957	SP
□ ○ Don Juans	Girl Of My Dreams	1959	SC
□ ○ **Doo-Wop All Stars**	**Lookin' For My Baby**	**1992**	**FN**
□ ○ **Dootones**	**Teller Of Fortune**	**1955**	**SC**
□ ○ Dorn, Jerry (w/the Hurricanes)	Wishing Well	1956	SP
□ ○ Dovells	Bristol Stomp	1961	FN
□ ○ Dovells	No No No	1961	FN
□ ○ **Dovells**	**Your Last Chance**	**1962**	**FC**
□ ○ Dovers, Miriam Grate & the	Sweet As A Flower	1959	SC /FL
□ ○ Dovers, Miriam Grate & the	Devil You May Be	1961	SC
□ ○ Dream Kings	More Than Yesterday, Less Than Tomorrow	1957	SC
□ ○ **Dreamers (A)**	**Melba**	**1955**	**SC**
□ ○ Dreamers (A)	Tears In My Eyes	1955	SC
□ ○ **Dreamers (B)**	**Teenage Vows Of Love**	**1960**	**MC**

☐○ **Dreamers (C), Donnie & the**	**My Memories Of You**	**1961**	**FN**
☐○ Dreamlovers	When We Get Married	1961	SN
☐○ **Dreamlovers**	**Zoom Zoom Zoom**	**1962**	**FC**
☐○ **Dreams**	**Darlene (Girl Of My Dreams)**	**1954**	**SP**
☐○ Drifters (A)	I'm The Caring Kind	1950	SP
☐○ Drifters (B)	Money Honey	1953	FP
☐○ Drifters (B)	The Way I Feel	1953	SP
☐○ Drifters (B)	Let The Boogie Woogie Roll	1953	FP
☐○ **Drifters (B)**	**Three Thirty Three**	**1953**	**FP**
☐○ Drifters (B)	Honey Love	1954	FP
☐○ Drifters (B)	Someday You'll Want Me To Want You	1954	SP
☐○ Drifters (B)	Such A Night	1954	FP
☐○ Drifters (B)	Warm Your Heart	1954	SP
☐○ Drifters (B)	White Christmas	1954	FP
☐○ **Drifters (B)**	**Lucille**	**1954**	**SP**
☐○ **Drifters (B)**	**Bip Bam**	**1954**	**FP**
☐○ **Drifters (B)**	**The Bells Of St. Mary's**	**1954**	**SP**
☐○ **Drifters (B)**	**Gone**	**1955**	**SP**
☐○ Drifters (B)	Adorable	1955	SP

□○ Drifters (B)	What'Cha Gonna Do	1955	FP
□○ Drifters (B)	Ruby Baby	1956	FP
□○ Drifters (B)	Your Promise To Be Mine	1956	SP
□○ **Drifters (B)**	**Fools Fall In Love**	**1957**	**FC**
□○ **Drifters (B)**	**Drip Drop**	**1958**	**FC**
□○ **Drifters (C)**	**Oh My Love**	**1959**	**SC**
□○ **Drifters (C)**	**Dance With Me**	**1959**	**MC**
□○ **Drifters (C)**	**(If You Cry) True Love, True Love**	**1959**	**MN**
□○ Drifters (C)	There Goes My Baby	1959	MN
□○ Drifters (C)	This Magic Moment	1959	MN
□○ Drifters (C)	Save The Last Dance For Me	1960	MN
□○ Drifters (C)	Sweets For My Sweet	1961	FN
□○ **Drifters (C)**	**Some Kind Of Wonderful**	**1961**	**MN**
□○ **Drifters (C)**	**Please Stay**	**1961**	**MN**
□○ **Drifters (C)**	**When My Little Girl Is Smiling**	**1962**	**FN**
□○ Drifters (C)	Up On The Roof	1962	MN
□○ **Drifters (C)**	**On Broadway**	**1963**	**MN**
□○ **Drifters (C)**	**Under The Boardwalk**	**1964**	**MN**

□○ **Du Droppers**	**Can't Do Sixty No More**	**1952**	**FP**
□○ Du Mauriers	All Night Long	1957	FC
□○ **Du Mauriers**	**Baby I Love You**	**1957**	**SC**
□○ Dubs	Could This Be Magic	1957	SC
□○ Dubs	Don't Ask Me (To Be Lonely)	1957	SC
□○ Dubs	Beside My Love	1958	SC
□○ Dubs	Chapel Of Dreams	1958	SC
□○ **Dubs**	**Be Sure My Love**	**1958**	**SC**
□○ Dubs	Is There A Love For Me	1958	SC
□○ **Dubs, Richard Blandon & the**	**Wherever You Are**	**1989**	**SC**
□○ **Ducanes**	**Little Did I Know**	**1961**	**SN**
□○ **Ducanes**	**I'm So Happy**	**1961**	**FN**
□○ **Dukes**	**Someday Somewhere (I'll Find Her)**	**1954**	**SC**
□○ **Dukes**	**Tear Drop Eyes**	**1956**	**SP**
□○ **Duponts**	**You**	**1956**	**SC**
□○ Duprees	My Own True Love	1962	SN
□○ Duprees	You Belong To Me	1962	SN
□○ **Duprees**	**Take Me As I Am**	**1962**	**SN**
□○ Duprees	Have Your Heard	1963	SN

83

□○ Duprees	Why Don't You Believe Me	1963	SN
□○ **Durhams**	**Maureen**	**1975**	**SC**
□○ **Duvals**	**You Came To Me**	**1956**	**SP**
□○ **Dynamics, Tony Maresco & the**	**Forever Love**	**1961**	**SN**
□○ Earls	Life Is But A Dream	1961	FN
□○ Earls	Lookin' For My Baby	1961	FN
□○ **Earls**	**Cross My Heart**	**1961**	**SN**
□○ **Earls**	**Without You**	**1961**	**SN**
□○ **Earls**	**My Heart's Desire**	**1961**	**FN**
□○ Earls	Eyes	1962	FN
□○ Earls	Remember Then	1962	FN
□○ Earls	Never	1963	FN
□○ Earls	I Believe	1964	SN
□○ **Earls**	**Remember Me Baby**	**1965**	**FN**
□○ **Earls**	**Dreams Come True**	**1973**	**FN**
□○ **Earls**	**Little Boy And Girl**	**1976**	**FN**
□○ **Earls**	**Lost Love**	**1976**	**SC**
□○ **Earls**	**All Through Our Teens**	**1976**	**SN**
□○ **Earth Angels**	**Come On Home**	**2010**	**SC**

☐○ **Earth Angels**	**Just One More Chance**	**2010**	**FC**
☐○ **Earth Angels**	**Look Into The Sky**	**2010**	**FC**
☐○ **Earth Angels**	**Nothing Can Go Wrong**	**2010**	**FC**
☐○ **Earth Angels**	**Weakness Acappella**	**2010**	**FC**
☐○ Ebb Tides, Nino & the	Jukebox Saturday Night	1961	FN
☐○ **Ebb Tides, Nino & the**	**Charlene**	**1961**	**SC**
☐○ **Ebb Tides, Nino & the**	**Those Oldies But Goodies (Remind Me Of You)**	**1961**	**SN**
☐○ **Ebbtides**	**What Is Your Name Dear?**	**1956**	**SC**
☐○ Ebonaires	Love Call	1959	SC
☐○ Echoes (A)	Ding Dong	1957	FC
☐○ Echoes (B)	Baby Blue	1961	FN
☐○ Edsels	What Brought Us Together	1960	SN
☐○ Edsels	Rama Lama Ding Dong	1961	FC
☐○ Edsels	Shake Shake Sherry	1962	FN
☐○ El Capris	Oh, But She Did	1956	FC
☐○ **El Cincos**	**Kiss Me**	**1957**	**FC**
☐○ El Domingos	Lucky Me, I'm In Love	1962	FN
☐○ **El Domingos**	**Made In Heaven**	**1962**	**SC**

□○ El Dorados	Baby I Need You	1954	SP
□○ El Dorados	At My Front Door	1955	FC
□○ El Dorados	I Began To Realize	1955	SC
□○ El Dorados	I'll Be Forever Loving You	1955	FC
□○ El Dorados	Bim Bam Boom	1956	FC
□○ **El Dorados**	**A Fallen Tear**	**1956**	**SC**
□○ El Dorados	There In The Night	1956	SP
□○ **El Sierros**	**Love You So**	**1964**	**FN**
□○ **El Torros**	**What's The Matter**	**1960**	**SC**
□○ **El Venos**	**Geraldine**	**1956**	**FC**
□○ **El Venos, Anne Keith & the**	**I Am Just A Lonely Girl**	**1959**	**SC/ FL**
□○ **El Venos**	**You Must (Won't) Be True**	**1957**	**SC/ FL**
□○ **El Venos**	**Now We're Together**	**1956**	**FC/ FL**
□○ **El Venos**	**My Heart Beats Faster**	**1957**	**FC/ FL**
□○ Elchords	Peppermint Stick	1957	FC
□○ **Elchords**	**Gee I'm In Love**	**1958**	**FC**
□○ Eldaros	Please Surrender	1958	SC

□○ Elegants	Goodnight	1958	SC
□○ Elegants	Little Star	1958	MC
□○ **Elegants**	**Getting Dizzy**	**1958**	**FC**
□○ **Elegants**	**Little Boy Blue (Is Blue No More)**	**1959**	**FC**
□○ **Elgins (A)**	**Uncle Sam's Man**	**1960**	**SC**
□○ Elgins (B)	Here In Your Arms	1964	SN
□○ **Elites**	**Northern Star**	**1965**	**FN**
□○ Embers (A)	Solitaire	1961	SC
□○ **Embers (B) (w/Gene Pitney)**	**Darkness**	**1959**	**FC**
□○ **Embers (B), Larry Lee & the**	**Winter Romance**	**1990**	**FC**
□○ **Emeralds**	**You're Driving Me Crazy**	**1959**	**SC**
□○ **Emeralds**	**Please Don't Crush My Dreams**	**1960**	**SC**
□○ Emblems, Patty & the	Mixed Up, Shook Up Girl	1964	FN /FG
□○ **Emotions (as the Motions)**	**Mr. Night**	**1961**	**FN**
□○ Emotions	Echo	1962	MN
□○ **Emotions**	**A Story Untold**	**1963**	**MN**

□○ **Enchanters (A)**	**Today Is Your Birthday**	**1952**	**SP/ FG**
□○ **Enchanters (B)**	**I Lied To My Heart**	**1961**	**SN**
□○ **Enchords**	**I Need You Baby**	**1961**	**SC**
□○ **Enchords**	**Zoom Zoom Zoom**	**1961**	**FC**
□○ Encounters	Don't Stop Now	1965	FN
□○ **Envoys**	**Springtime**	**1963**	**SN**
□○ Ermines	I'm So Used To You Now	1956	FC
□○ **Ervin, Frankie (bb/Shields)**	**Some Other Guy**	**1960**	**SC**
□○ **Escorts**	**Gaudeamus**	**1962**	**FN**
□○ **Escorts, Del & the**	**Baby Doll**	**1961**	**FN/ FL**
□○ **Esquires**	**Only The Angels Know**	**1957**	**SP**
□○ Essentials, Billy & the	Maybe You'll Be There	1962	FN
□○ **Essentials, Billy & the**	**Babalu's Wedding Day**	**1966**	**FN**
□○ Essex	A Walkin' Miracle	1963	FN /FL
□○ Essex	Easier Said Than Done	1963	FN /FL
□○ Eternals	Babalu's Wedding Day	1959	FC

□○ Eternals	My Girl	1959	SC
□○ Eternals	Rockin' In The Jungle	1959	FC
□○ **Eternals**	**Rock 'n' Roll Cha Cha**	**1959**	**MN**
□○ **Everglades, Johnny Banks & the**	**While Sitting In The Chapel**	**1961**	**SC**
□○ **Evergreens (A)**	**Very Truly Yours**	**1955**	**SC**
□○ Evergreens, (B) Dante & the	Alley Oop	1960	FN
□○ Excellents	Coney Island Baby	1962	SN
□○ **Excellents**	**Helene (Your Wish Came True)**	**1964**	**SN**
□○ **Excellents**	**You Baby You**	**1962**	**FN**
□○ **Excellents**	**Love No One But You**	**1963**	**SC**
□○ **Excellons**	**Sunday Kind Of Love**	**1964**	**FN**
□○ **Exceptions**	**Down By The Ocean**	**1963**	**FN**
□○ **Exodus**	**M&M**	**1972**	**FN**
□○ **Exotics**	**My Heart Belongs To Only You**	**1959**	**SC**
□○ **Explorers**	**I'm Simply Asking You**	**1959**	**SC**
□○ Explorers, Dennis & the	Vision Of Love	1960	SN
□○ **Explorers**	**Don't Be A Fool**	**1960**	**SN**

89

☐○ **Extremes**	**Come Next Spring**	**1958**	**SC**
☐○ Fabulaires	While Walking	1957	FC
☐○ **Fabulaires**	**No No**	**1957**	**SC**
☐○ **Fabulons**	**Rene**	**1960**	**SN**
☐○ **Fabulons**	**I Only Want You**	**1961**	**FC**
☐○ **Fabulons**	**Smoke From Your Cigarette**	**1960**	**SC**
☐○ **Fabulous Dudes**	**Ding Dong Darling**	**1994**	**FN**
☐○ **Fabulous Dudes**	**Betty Blue Moon**	**1994**	**FN**
☐○ **Fabulous Pearl Devines**	**So Lonely**	**1959**	**SC**
☐○ Fabulous Pearl Devines	You've Been Gone	1959	FC
☐○ **Fabulous Pearls**	**I Laughed So Hard**	**1959**	**FC**
☐○ Fabulous Twilights, Nathaniel Mayer &	Village Of Love	1962	FN
☐○ Falcons	You're So Fine	1959	FC
☐○ Fantastics	There Goes My Love	1959	SC
☐○ **Fantastics**	**Dancing Doll**	**1961**	**SC**
☐○ **Fantastics**	**My Girls**	**1990**	**SC**

□○ **Fascinations, Jordan & the**	**My Imagination**	**1961**	**SN**
□○ **Fascinations, Jordan & the**	**Once Upon A Time**	**1961**	**FN**
□○ **Fascinations Jordan & the**	**Goodnight**	**1962**	**SN**
□○ Fascinators (A)	My Beauty, My Own	1954	SP
□○ Fascinators (B)	Chapel Bells	1958	SC
□○ Fascinators (B)	Wonder Who	1958	FC
□○ Fascinators (B)	Oh Rose Marie	1959	FC
□○ Fascinators (B)	Who Do You Think You Are	1959	SC
□○ **Fascinators (C) (aka Five Boroughs)**	**Gloria, My Love**	**1996**	**SC**
□○ Fashions	I'm Dreaming Of You	1959	FC /FL
□○ **Fashions**	**I Love You So**	**1959**	**FC**
□○ Feathers	Johnny, Darling	1954	SP
□○ **Federals**	**Come Go With Me**	**1957**	**FC**
□○ Fi-Tones	Foolish Dreams	1957	SC
□○ Fi-Tones	My Faith	1957	SC
□○ Fi-Tones Quintette	It Wasn't A Lie	1955	SC
□○ Fidelitys	The Things I Love	1958	SC

□○ Fiestas	Last Night I Dreamed	1958	SC
□○ Fiestas	So Fine	1958	FC
□○ **Fiestas**	**Things We Can't Forget**	**1959**	**FC**
□○ Fiestas	The Hobo's Prayer	1961	SC
□○ Fireflies	I Can't Say Goodbye	1959	SC
□○ Fireflies	You Were Mine	1959	SN
□○ **Five (5) Arcades**	**Hoping You'll Fall In Love**	**1973**	**SP**
□○ **Five Bell Aires, Henry Hall & the**	**I'm So Happy**	**1959**	**SC**
□○ **Five Bell Aires, Henry Hall & the**	**House Of Love**	**1959**	**FC**
□○ **Five Bell Aires, John Hall & the**	**Wedding Bells**	**1959**	**FC**
□○ **Five Bell Aires, John Hall & the**	**Come On Home**	**1959**	**MC**
□○ Five Blue Notes	The Beat Of Our Hearts	1954	SP
□○ **Five Boroughs**	**Heaven And Cindy**	**1990**	**SC**
□○ **Five Chancells**	**Love No One But You**	**1965**	**SC**
□○ Five Chances	All I Want	1955	SP
□○ Five Chances	Gloria	1956	SC
□○ **Five Chums**	**Give Me The Power**	**1957**	**SP**

☐○ Five Crowns	Lullaby Of The Bells	1952	SP
☐○ Five Crowns	You Came To Me	1955	SP
☐○ **Five Delights**	**There'll Be No Goodbye**	**1958**	**SC**
☐○ **Five Delights**	**Whatcha Gonna Do**	**1960**	**FC**
☐○ Five Discs	I Remember	1958	FC
☐○ **Five Discs**	**The World Is A Beautiful Place**	**1958**	**SC**
☐○ **Five Discs**	**Come On Baby**	**1961**	**FN**
☐○ Five Discs	Adios	1961	FN
☐○ Five Discs	My Baby Loves Me	1961	SN
☐○ Five Discs	Never Let You Go	1961	FN
☐○ Five Discs	That Was The Time	1962	SN
☐○ **Five Dollars**	**Harmony Of Love**	**1955**	**SC**
☐○ Five Dollars	That's The Way It Goes	1960	SC
☐○ Five Embers	Please Come Home	1954	SP
☐○ Five Emeralds	Darling	1954	SP
☐○ Five Emeralds	I'll Beg	1954	SP
☐○ Five Keys	Glory Of Love	1951	SP
☐○ Five Keys	With A Broken Heart	1951	SP
☐○ Five Keys	Red Sails In The Sunset	1952	SP
☐○ **Five Keys**	**Yes Sir, That's My Baby**	**1952**	**SP**

93

□○ **Five Keys**	**Mistakes**	**1952**	**SP**
□○ **Five Keys**	**My Saddest Hour**	**1953**	**SP**
□○ Five Keys	These Foolish Things	1953	SP
□○ Five Keys	Deep In My Heart	1954	SP
□○ Five Keys	Ling Ting Tong	1954	FP
□○ Five Keys	Close Your Eyes	1955	SP
□○ Five Keys	I Wish I'd Never Learned To Read	1955	SP
□○ Five Keys	The Verdict	1955	SP
□○ Five Keys	Out Of Sight, Out Of Mind	1956	SP
□○ Five Keys	Wisdom Of A Fool	1956	SP
□○ **Five Kings**	**Dear Lord**	**2000**	**SC**
□○ **Five Notes**	**Park Your Love**	**1955**	**SC**
□○ **Five Notes**	**Show Me The Way**	**1955**	**SC**
□○ Five Notes	You Are So Beautiful	1955	SC
□○ Five Notes	Show Me The Way	1956	SC
□○ **Five Owls**	**Pleading To You**	**1955**	**SC**
□○ **Five Pearls (aka Pearls)**	**Please Let Me Know**	**1954**	**SC**
□○ **Five Pearls (aka Pearls)**	**Real Humdinger**	**1954**	**FC**

□○ Five Royales	Give Me One More Chance	1951	SP
□○ **Five Royales**	**Crazy Crazy Crazy**	**1953**	**FP**
□○ Five Royales	My Wants For Love	1956	SP
□○ Five Royales	Dedicated To The One I Love	1957	SP
□○ Five Satins	I Remember (In The Still Of The Night)	1956	SC
□○ Five Satins	Wonderful Girl	1956	SC
□○ **Five Satins**	**All Mine**	**1956**	**SC**
□○ **Five Satins**	**Baby Face**	**1956**	**SC**
□○ Five Satins	Oh Happy Day	1957	SC
□○ Five Satins	Our Anniversary	1957	SC
□○ Five Satins	To The Aisle	1957	SC
□○ Five Satins	Wishing Ring	1961	SN
□○ **Five Secrets**	**Ding Dong Teenage Bells**	**1957**	**FC**
□○ Five Sharps	Stormy Weather	1952	SP
□○ **Five Trojans**	**Alone In This World**	**1958**	**FC**
□○ **Five Trojans (Nicky St. Clair & the)**	**I Hear Those Bells**	**1959**	**FN**
□○ **Five Vets**	**Right Now**	**1956**	**FC**
□○ **Five Willows**	**Do You Love Me**	**1956**	**FC**
□○ Flairs	This Is The Night For Love	1954	SP

☐ ○ Flairs, Cornel Gunter & the	She Wants To Rock	1956	FC
☐ ○ **Flames, Carroll Pegues & the**	**Darling Jane**	**1962**	**SC**
☐ ○ **Flaming Hearts**	**Baby**	**1958**	**SC**
☐ ○ Flamingos	Golden Teardrops	1953	SP
☐ ○ Flamingos	If I Can't Have You	1953	SP
☐ ○ Flamingos	Someday Someway	1953	FP
☐ ○ **Flamingos**	**That's My Desire**	**1953**	**SP**
☐ ○ **Flamingos**	**Plan For Love**	**1953**	**SP**
☐ ○ Flamingos	Dream Of A Lifetime	1954	SP
☐ ○ Flamingos	Jump Children	1954	FP
☐ ○ **Flamingos**	**Cross Over The Bridge**	**1954**	**SP**
☐ ○ **Flamingos**	**I'm Yours**	**1955**	**SC**
☐ ○ **Flamingos**	**The Vow**	**1955**	**SC**
☐ ○ Flamingos	A Kiss From Your Lips	1956	SP
☐ ○ Flamingos	I'll Be Home	1956	SP
☐ ○ Flamingos	Lovers Never Say Goodbye	1958	SC
☐ ○ Flamingos	I Only Have Eyes For You	1959	SC
☐ ○ Flamingos	Mio Amore	1960	SC
☐ ○ Flamingos	Nobody Loves Me Like You Do	1960	FN

□ ○ Fleetwoods	Come Softly To Me	1959	MN
□ ○ Fleetwoods	Mr. Blue	1959	MN
□ ○ **Fleetwoods**	**Tragedy**	**1961**	**SN**
□ ○ Flips (Little Joey & the)	Bongo Stomp	1962	FN
□ ○ Four Bars	If I Give My Heart To You	1954	SP
□ ○ Four Buddies	I Will Wait	1951	SP
□ ○ Four Buddies	Just To See You Smile Again	1951	SP
□ ○ Four Buddies	Simply Say Goodbye	1951	SP
□ ○ Four Buddies	Why At A Time Like This	1951	SP
□ ○ **Four Buddies**	**Sweet Slumber**	**1951**	**SP**
□ ○ **Four Buddies**	**Heart And Soul**	**1951**	**SP**
□ ○ Four Buddies	You're Part Of Me	1952	SP
□ ○ Four Deuces	W-P-L-J	1955	FP
□ ○ **Four Evers**	**Be My Girl**	**1964**	**FN**
□ ○ **Four Dots, Jerry Stone & the**	**My Baby**	**1958**	**SC**
□ ○ Four Dots, Jerry Stone & the	Pleading For Your Love	1959	SC
□ ○ Four Fellows	Angels Say	1955	SP
□ ○ Four Fellows	In The Rain	1955	SP
□ ○ Four Fellows	Soldier Boy	1955	SP

97

□○ Four Fellows	Darling You	1956	SP
□○ Four Fellows	You Don't Know Me	1956	SP
□○ **Four Fellows**	**Loving You Darling**	**1956**	**FC**
□○ Four Fellows	Give Me Back My Broken Heart	1957	SP
□○ Four Flames	Tabarin	1951	SP
□○ **Four Gabriels**	**Gloria**	**1948**	**SP**
□○ Four Haven Knights	In My Lonely Room	1956	FC
□○ Four Haven Knights	Just To Be In Love	1957	SC
□○ **Four Haven Knights**	**Why Go On Pretending**	**1958**	**SC**
□○ **Four Knights**	**La La**	**1962**	**FN**
□○ Four J's	Here I Am Broken Hearted	1964	FN
□○ **Four Lovers**	**You're The Apple Of My Eye**	**1956**	**FC**
□○ **Four Most**	**I Love You**	**1959**	**FC**
□○ **Four Seasons**	**Marlena**	**1963**	**FN**
□○ G-Clefs	'Cause You're Mine	1956	FC
□○ G-Clefs	Darla My Darling	1956	FC
□○ G-Clefs	Ka Ding Dong	1956	FC
□○ G-Clefs	Symbol Of Love	1957	SC

☐○ **G-Clefs**	**I Understand**	**1961**	**SC**
☐○ Gardenias	Flaming Love	1956	FC
☐○ Gay Knights	The Loudness Of My Heart	1958	SC
☐○ **Gaytunes**	**Thrill Of Romance**	**1953**	**SP**
☐○ Gaytunes	I Love You	1957	SC
☐○ Gaytunes	Plea In The Moonlight	1958	FC
☐○ Gazelles	Honest	1956	SC
☐○ Gems	'Deed I Do	1954	SP
☐○ Gems	You're Tired Of Love	1954	SP
☐○ Genies	Who's That Knockin'	1959	FC
☐○ Gentlemen	Don't Leave Me Baby	1954	FC
☐○ **Gentlemen**	**Something To Remember You By**	**1954**	**FP**
☐○ **Gents**	**I'll Never Let You Go**	**1964**	**FN**
☐○ **Girlfriends, Erlene & Her**	**Because Of You**	**1963**	**SN/ FG**
☐○ Gladiators	Girl Of My Heart	1957	SC
☐○ Gladiolas	Little Darlin'	1957	FC
☐○ **Gladiolas**	**Hey Little Girl**	**1958**	**FC**
☐○ **Gladiolas**	**Shoop Shoop**	**1958**	**FC**
☐○ Globetrotters	Rainy Day Bells	1970	FC

□ ○ Goldentones	The Meaning Of Love	1955	SC
□ ○ Greco, Johnny (& group)	Rocket Ride	1963	FN
□ ○ Greene, Barbara (& group)	Long Tall Sally	1963	FN /FL
□ ○ **Guys, Little Sammy Rozzi & the**	**Over The Rainbow**	**1963**	**FN**
□ ○ Guytones	This Is Love	1957	FC
□ ○ **Guytones**	**Hunky Dory**	**1957**	**FC**
□ ○ Halos	Nag	1961	FN
□ ○ **Halos**	**Crazy Bells**	**1962**	**FN**
□ ○ **Hamber, Kenny & group**	**Tears In My Eyes**	**1960**	**SN**
□ ○ Harmonaires	Come Back	1957	FC
□ ○ Harmonaires	Lorraine	1957	SC
□ ○ Harptones	A Sunday Kind Of Love	1953	SP
□ ○ **Harptones**	**I'll Never Tell**	**1953**	**SP**
□ ○ Harptones	Life Is But A Dream	1954	SP
□ ○ Harptones	Loving A Girl Like You	1954	SP
□ ○ Harptones	My Memories Of You	1954	SP
□ ○ Harptones	Since I Fell For You	1954	SP
□ ○ **Harptones**	**My Success (It All Depends On You)**	**1955**	**SP**

□○ **Harptones**	**What Is Your Decision**	**1956**	**SP**
□○ **Harptones**	**The Masquerade Is Over**	**1956**	**SP**
□○ Harptones	On Sunday Afternoon	1956	SP
□○ Harptones	That's The Way It Goes	1956	SP
□○ Harptones	Three Wishes	1956	SP
□○ Harptones	Cry Like I Cried	1957	SP
□○ Harptones	The Shrine Of St. Cecilia	1957	SP
□○ **Harptones**	**Foolish Me**	**1961**	**SC**
□○ Harris, Thurston (w/the Sharps)	Little Bitty Pretty One	1957	FC
□○ **Hart, Rocky & the Passions**	**Every Day**	**1959**	**FC**
□○ **Headhunters, Cannibal & the**	**I'll Show You How To Love Me**	**1965**	**SN**
□○ **Headliners, George Goodman & the**	**Let Me Love You**	**1964**	**SN**
□○ **Heard, Lonnie (bb/5 Dollars)**	**Sunday Kind Of Love**	**1961**	**FN**
□○ Heart Beats Quintet (aka Heartbeats)	Tormented	1955	SC
□○ Heartbeats	A Thousand Miles Away	1956	SC
□○ Heartbeats	Crazy For You	1956	SC
□○ Heartbeats	Darling How Long	1956	SC

□○ Heartbeats	Oh Baby Don't	1956	FC
□○ Heartbeats	People Are Talking	1956	SC
□○ Heartbeats	Rock 'n' Rollin' 'n' Rhythm ' n' Blues-n'	1956	FC
□○ Heartbeats	Your Way	1956	SC
□○ **Heartbeats**	**I Won't Be The Fool Any More**	**1957**	**SC**
□○ **Heartbeats**	**Everybody's Somebody's Fool**	**1957**	**SC**
□○ Heartbeats	Down On My Knees	1958	SC
□○ **Heartbeats**	**One Day Next Year**	**1958**	**SC**
□○ **Heartbeats**	**One Million Years**	**1959**	**SC**
□○ Heartbreakers (A)	Heartbreaker	1951	SP
□○ Heartbreakers (B)	Without A Cause	1957	FC
□○ **Heartbreakers (B)**	**1, 2, I Love You**	**1957**	**FC**
□○ **Heartbreakers (B)**	**Come Back My Love**	**1957**	**FC**
□○ Hearts (A), Lee Andrews & the	Maybe You'll Be There	1954	SP
□○ **Hearts (A), Lee Andrews & the**	**The White Cliffs Of Dover**	**1954**	**SP**
□○ **Hearts (A), Lee Andrews & the**	**The Bells Of St. Mary's**	**1954**	**SP**
□○ **Hearts (A), Lee Andrews & the**	**The Fairest**	**1954**	**SP**

□○ Hearts (A), Lee Andrews & the	Bluebird Of Happiness	1956	SP
□○ Hearts (A), Lee Andrews & the	Lonely Room	1956	SC
□○ **Hearts (A), Lee Andrews & the**	**Just Suppose**	**1956**	**SC**
□○ Hearts (A), Lee Andrews & the	Long Lonely Nights	1957	SP
□○ Hearts (A), Lee Andrews & the	Teardrops	1957	SP
□○ Hearts (A), Lee Andrews & the	The Clock	1957	FC
□○ **Hearts (A), Lee Andrews & the**	**Girl Around The Corner**	**1957**	**FC**
□○ Hearts (A), Lee Andrews & the	Try The Impossible	1958	SP
□○ Hearts (A), Lee Andrews & the	Why Do I	1958	SP
□○ Hearts (A), Lee Andrews & the	I'm Sorry Pillow	1963	SP
□○ Hearts (B)	Lonely Nights	1955	SC /FG
□○ Hearts (B)	He Drives Me Crazy	1956	SC /FG
□○ **Heartspinners, Dino & the**	**The Flame**	**1983**	**SC**

□○ **Heartspinners, Dino & the**	**Who Do You Think You Are**	**1972**	**SC**
□○ Hemlocks, Little Bobby Rivera & the	Cora Lee	1957	FC
□○ **Hemlocks, Little Bobby Rivera & the**	**The Joys Of Love**	**1957**	**SC**
□○ Hi-Fives	Dorothy	1958	FC
□○ Hi-Lites (A), Ronnie & the	I Wish That We Were Married	1962	SN
□○ **Hi-Lites (B)**	**Walking My Baby Back Home**	**1961**	**FC**
□○ **Hi-Lites (B)**	**I'm Falling In Love**	**1961**	**MC**
□○ **Hi-Lites (B)**	**Zoop**	**1962**	**FC**
□○ **Hi-Lites (B)**	**Everybody's Somebody's Fool**	**1962**	**SC**
□○ **Hi-Lites (B)**	**Zoom Zoom Zoom**	**1962**	**FC**
□○ **Hi-Lites (B)**	**Maybe You'll Be There**	**1962**	**SC**
□○ **Hi-Lites (B)**	**To The Aisle**	**1962**	**SC**
□○ **Hi-Lites (B)**	**For Your Precious Love**	**1962**	**SC**
□○ Hi-Lites (B)	Gloria (My Darling)	1962	SN
□○ Hi-Lites (B)	Pretty Face	1962	SN
□○ Hide-A-Ways	Can't Help Loving That Girl Of Mine	1954	SP

□○ **Hide-A-Ways**	**Cherie**	**1954**	**SC**
□○ **High Hatters**	**It's You**	**1961**	**SN**
□○ Hits, Tiny Tim & the	Wedding Bells	1958	SC
□○ **Holidays**	**One Little Kiss**	**1961**	**SN**
□○ **Hollywood Flames**	**I Know**	**1953**	**SC**
□○ Hollywood Flames	Peggy	1954	SP
□○ Hollywood Flames	Buzz Buzz Buzz	1957	FC
□○ Hollywood Flames	Just For You	1959	SC
□○ **Hollywood Four Flames**	**Tabarin**	**1951**	**SP**
□○ **Hollywood Saxons**	**Is It True?**	**1958**	**SC**
□○ **Hollywood Saxons**	**Everyday's A Holiday**	**1961**	**SC**
□○ Hornets	Crying Over You	1957	SC
□○ **Howard, Gregory (bb/Cadillacs)**	**When In Love**	**1963**	**FN**
□○ **Hummers**	**Gee What A Girl**	**1956**	**FP**
□○ **Hurricanes**	**Pistol Packin' Mama**	**1955**	**FC**
□○ Hurricanes	Dear Mother	1956	SC

☐○ Hurricanes	Maybe It's All For The Best	1956	SC
☐○ **Hurricanes**	**Little Girl Of Mine**	**1956**	**FC**
☐○ **Hurricanes**	**Your Promise To Me (aka ...To Be Mine)**	**1956**	**SC**
☐○ **Hurricanes**	**It's Raining In My Heart**	**1956**	**SC**
☐○ Hurricanes	Fallen Angel	1957	SC
☐○ Hurricanes	Priceless	1957	SC
☐○ **Hy-Tones**	**I'm A Fool**	**1959**	**SC**
☐○ **Ikettes**	**I'm Blue (The Gong Gong Song)**	**1962**	**FN /FG**
☐○ **Illusions**	**Hey Boy**	**1962**	**FN**
☐○ Imaginations	Hey You	1961	SN
☐○ **Imaginations**	**Guardian Angel**	**1961**	**FC**
☐○ **Imaginations**	**Good Night Baby**	**1961**	**FN**
☐○ Imaginations	Mystery Of You	1961	FN
☐○ Imaginations	The Search Is Over	1961	SN
☐○ **Imaginations**	**Never Let You Go**	**1976**	**SN**
☐○ Impalas	Sorry (I Ran All The Way Home)	1959	FC
☐○ Imperials (A)	My Darling	1952	SP
☐○ Imperials (B), Little Anthony & the	So Much	1958	SC

□○ Imperials (B), Little Anthony & the	Tears On My Pillow	1958	SC
□○ Imperials (B), Little Anthony &	Two People In The World	1958	SC
□○ **Imperials (B), Little Anthony & the**	**The Diary**	**1958**	**SC**
□○ **Imperials (B), Little Anthony & the**	**Wishful Thinking**	**1959**	**SC**
□○ **Imperials (B), Little Anthony & the**	**A Prayer And A Jukebox**	**1959**	**SC**
□○ Imperials (B), Little Anthony & the	Shimmy, Shimmy Ko-Ko-Bop	1959	MC
□○ Imperials (B), Little Anthony & the	When You Wish Upon A Star	1959	SC
□○ Imperials (B), Little Anthony & the	Traveling Stranger	1961	FC
□○ **Impossibles, Linda Carr & the**	**Shy One**	**1961**	**SN /FL**
□○ Impressions, Jerry Butler & the	For Your Precious Love	1958	SN
□○ **Impressions, Jerry Butler & the**	**Come Back My Love**	**1958**	**SC**
□○ **Incredible Upsetters**	**Oo-Wah-Cha-Wah**	**1959**	**FC**
□○ **Incredible Upsetters**	**My Life, My Loved One**	**1959**	**SC**

☐○ **Indigos**	**Woo Woo Pretty Girl**	**1961**	**FN**
☐○ **Infascinations**	**I'm So In Love**	**1961**	**SC**
☐○ **Infatuators**	**I Found My Love**	**1961**	**FN**
☐○ **Infatuators**	**Where Are You**	**1961**	**SN**
☐○ Initials, Angelo & the	Bells Of Joy	1959	SC
☐○ **Inquisitors, Little Isidore & the**	**Why Do You Cry**	**1995**	**SN**
☐○ **Inquisitors, Little Isidore & the**	**Bongo Stomp**	**1995**	**FN**
☐○ **Inquisitors, Little Isidore & the**	**All Nite Long**	**1996**	**FN**
☐○ **Innocents**	**Gee Whiz**	**1961**	**SC**
☐○ **Innocents, Kathy Young & the**	**A Thousand Stars**	**1960**	**SC**
☐○ **Inspirations**	**Dry Your Eyes**	**1956**	**SC**
☐○ **Inspirators**	**If Loving You Is Wrong**	**1955**	**SP**
☐○ **Intentions**	**Summertime Angel**	**1963**	**FN**
☐○ **Interiors**	**Darling Little Angel**	**1961**	**SC**
☐○ **Intervals**	**Here's That Rainy Day**	**1962**	**SN**

□○ Isley Brothers	The Cow Jumped Over The Moon	1956	FC
□○ **Ivorys**	**Why Don't You Write Me**	**1962**	**SC**
□○ Ivy-Tones	Oo-Wee Baby	1958	FC
□○ Jacks	Why Don't You Write Me	1955	SP
□○ **Jacks**	**Away**	**1955**	**SC**
□○ Jacks	Why Did I Fall In Love	1956	SC
□○ **Jacks**	**Hands Across The Table**	**1957**	**SP**
□○ Jaguars	The Way You Look Tonight	1956	SP
□○ **Jaguars**	**Thinking Of You**	**1959**	**SC**
□○ **Jaguars**	**Play A Love Song**	**1990**	**SC**
□○ Jamies	Summertime, Summertime	1958	FC /FL
□○ **Januarys, Little June & His**	**Hello**	**1957**	**SC**
□○ **Januarys, Little June & His**	**Oh What A Feeling**	**1958**	**SC**
□○ Jayhawks	Stranded In The Jungle	1956	FC
□○ **Jayhawks**	**Counting My Teardrops**	**1956**	**SC**
□○ **Jaynells**	**Out Of A Million Girls**	**1984**	**SN**
□○ **Jaynells**	**Hollywood Actor**	**1984**	**FN**
□○ Jaytones	Oh Darling	1958	FC

109

☐○ **Jaytones**	**The Clock**	**1958**	**SC**
☐○ Jelly Beans	I Wanna Love Him So Bad	1964	FN /FG
☐○ **Jelly Beans**	**The Kind Of Boy You Can't Forget**	**1964**	**FN/ FG**
☐○ Jesters	I'm Falling In Love	1957	FC
☐○ Jesters	Love No One But You	1957	SC
☐○ Jesters	Please Let Me Love You	1957	SC
☐○ Jesters	So Strange	1957	SC
☐○ Jesters	I Laughed	1958	FC
☐○ Jesters	Now That You're Gone	1958	SC
☐○ Jesters	Oh Baby	1958	FC
☐○ Jesters	The Plea	1958	SC
☐○ **Jesters**	**The Wind**	**1960**	**SC**
☐○ Jets	Heaven Above Me	1956	FC
☐○ Jewels	Hearts Of Stone	1954	FP
☐○ **Jewels**	**Hearts Can Be Broken**	**1955**	**FC**
☐○ Jive Bombers	Bad Boy	1957	SP
☐○ Jive Five	My True Story	1961	SN
☐○ Jive Five	Never, Never	1961	SN
☐○ Jive Five	These Golden Rings	1962	SN

□○ Jive Five	What Time Is It	1962	SN
□○ **Jive Five**	**No Not Again**	**1962**	**SN**
□○ **Jive Five**	**I'm A Happy Man**	**1965**	**FN**
□○ **Jive Five**	**Where Do We Go From Here**	**1982**	**SN**
□○ **Jo-Ann & group**	**Baby Doll**	**1961**	**FN/ FL**
□○ **Joel, Billy**	**For The Longest Time**	**1984**	**FN**
□○ Johnson, Herb (bb/Cruisers)	Have You Heard	1960	MN
□○ **Jones, Jimmy (bb/Cues)**	**Handy Man**	**1960**	**FC**
□○ Joytones	My Foolish Heart	1956	SC /FG
□○ **Juniors (A), Jimmy Castor & the**	**I Promise To Remember**	**1956**	**FC**
□○ **Juniors (A), Jimmy Castor & the**	**I Know The Meaning Of Love**	**1956**	**SC**
□○ **Juniors (A), Jimmy Castor & the**	**This Girl Of Mine**	**1957**	**FC**
□○ Juniors (A), Jimmy Castor &	Somebody Mentioned Your Your Name	1957	SC
□○ Juniors (B), Danny & the	At The Hop	1957	FC

☐○ Juniors (B), Danny & the	Sometimes When I'm All Alone	1957	SC
☐○ Juniors (B), Danny & the	Rock And Roll Is Here To Stay	1957	FC
☐○ **Juniors (B), Danny & the**	**Schoolboy Romance**	**1957**	**SC**
☐○ **Juniors (B), Danny & the**	**Dottie**	**1958**	**FC**
☐○ **Juniors (B), Danny & the**	**Twistin' U.S.A.**	**1960**	**FC**
☐○ Kac-Ties	Happy Birthday	1963	SC
☐○ **Kac-Ties**	**Girl In My Heart**	**1963**	**FC**
☐○ **Keens, Rick & the**	**Peanuts**	**1961**	**FN**
☐○ **Keens, Rick & the**	**Darla**	**1964**	**FN**
☐○ **Keynotes**	**I Don't Know (Why I Love You Like I Do)**	**1955**	**FC**
☐○ **Keynotes**	**Now I Know**	**1956**	**FC**
☐○ **Keynotes**	**Zup Zup (Ooh You Dance So Nice)**	**1956**	**FC**
☐○ Keynotes	In The Evening	1956	FC
☐○ Keynotes	Really Wish You Were Here	1956	FC
☐○ Keynotes	One Little Kiss	1957	SC

□○ Keystoners	Sleep And Dream	1961	FC
□○ **Keystoners**	**Magic Kiss**	**1956**	**FC**
□○ **Keystoners**	**Gossip**	**1992**	**FC**
□○ **Keystoners**	**Them There Eyes**	**1992**	**FC**
□○ Keytones	Seven Wonders Of The World	1957	SC
□○ **Kidds**	**Are You Forgetting Me**	**1955**	**SP**
□○ **Killers, Hank Blackman & the**	**Everyone Has Someone**	**1962**	**SN**
□○ **King, Clydie & group**	**Our Romance**	**1957**	**SC/ FL**
□○ King Crooners	Now That She's Gone	1959	SC
□○ King Crooners	She's Mine All Mine	1959	FC
□○ King Crooners	Won't You Let Me Know	1959	FC
□○ **King Crooners**	**Pretty Little Girl**	**1959**	**FC**
□○ **King Crooners**	**School Daze**	**1960**	**FC**
□○ **King Crooners**	**Memoirs**	**1960**	**SC**
□○ **Kings, Bobby Hall & the**	**Sunday Kind Of Love**	**1953**	**SP**
□○ **Kings Men**	**Don't Say You're Sorry**	**1957**	**SP**
□○ **Klein, Robert & group**	**Fabulous 50's**	**1973**	**SN**

113

□○ Knockouts	Darling Lorraine	1959	SC
□○ Kodaks (aka Kodoks)	Little Boy And Girl	1957	FC /FL
□○ Kodaks (aka Kodoks)	Oh Gee, Oh Gosh	1957	FC /FL
□○ **Kodaks (aka Kodoks)**	**Make Believe World**	**1957**	**SC/ FL**
□○ Kodaks (aka Kodoks)	Teenager' s Dream	1957	SC /FL
□○ Kodaks (aka Kodoks)	Runaround Baby	1960	FC /FL
□○ **Kodaks (aka Kodoks)**	**Guardian Angel**	**1960**	**SC/ FL**
□○ Kool Gents	This Is The Night	1956	SC
□○ **Kool Gents**	**I Can't Help Myself**	**1956**	**SC**
□○ **Kool Gents**	**Just Like A Fool**	**1974**	**SC**
□○ Kuf-Linx	So Tough	1958	FC
□○ Ladders	Counting The Stars	1957	FC
□○ **Ladders**	**I Want To Know**	**1957**	**SC**
□○ **Ladders**	**My Love Is Gone**	**1959**	**SC**
□○ Laddins	Did It	1957	FC
□○ Laddins	Yes, Oh Baby Yes	1959	FC
□○ Lamplighters	I Used To Cry Mercy, Mercy	1954	FP

□○ **Lancers**	**Oh Little Girl**	**1963**	**FN**
□○ **Landis, Jerry & group**	**Lone Teen Ranger**	**1962**	**FN**
□○ **Lanes**	**Open Up Your Heart**	**1956**	**FC**
□○ **Lanham, Richard (w/Tempo-Tones)**	**On Your Radio**	**1955**	**FC**
□○ **Lar-Kings**	**Ship Of Love**	**1997**	**SC**
□○ **Larados**	**Now The Parting Begins**	**1957**	**SC**
□○ Larks (A)	Hopefully Yours	1951	SP
□○ Larks (A)	My Reverie	1951	SP
□○ **Larks (A)**	**I Live True To You**	**1952**	**SP**
□○ Larks (A)	Darlin'	1952	SP
□○ Larks (A)	In My Lonely Room	1952	SP
□○ Larks (A)	If It's A Crime	1954	SP
□○ Larks (B) (w/ Don Julian)	There Is A Girl	1961	FN
□○ **Latin Lads, Julito & the**	**Nunca (Never)**	**1963**	**FN**
□○ **Laurels**	**You Left Me**	**1959**	**SC**
□○ **Laurels**	**Baby Talk**	**1959**	**FC**
□○ Leaders	Stormy Weather	1955	SP

☐○ Lee, Curtis (bb/Halos)	Pretty Little Angel Eyes	1961	FN
☐○ Legends	I'll Never Fall In Love Again	1957	FC
☐○ Legends	The Legend Of Love	1958	SC
☐○ **Legends Of Doo-Wop**	**Chapel Bells**	**1998**	**SC**
☐○ **Legends Of Doo-Wop**	**I Wonder Who**	**1998**	**FC**
☐○ **Legends Of Doo-Wop**	**Hey You**	**1998**	**SC**
☐○ **Legends Of Doo-Wop**	**Mystery Of You**	**1998**	**FC**
☐○ **Legends Of Doo-Wop**	**Oh Rosemarie**	**1998**	**FC**
☐○ **Legends Of Doo-Wop**	**Guardian Angel**	**1998**	**FC**
☐○ **Legends Of Doo-Wop**	**This Is My Love**	**1998**	**SC**
☐○ **Legends Of Doo-Wop**	**Who Do You Think You Are**	**1998**	**SC**
☐○ **Legends Of Doo-Wop**	**I Only Want You**	**1998**	**FC**
☐○ **Legends Of Doo-Wop**	**Just To Be With You**	**1998**	**SC**

□○ **Lewis, Bobby & group**	**Tossin' And Turnin'**	**1961**	**FN/ FG**
□○ Lexingtons, Joey & the	Bobbie	1963	FN
□○ Limelighters	Cabin Hideaway	1956	FC
□○ Limelights, Shep & the	Daddy's Home	1961	SC
□○ Limelights, Shep & the	Our Anniversary	1962	SC
□○ Limelights, Shep & the	Three Steps To The Altar	1962	SC
□○ **Limelights, Shep & the**	**What Did Daddy Do**	**1962**	**SN**
□○ **Lions, Lugee & the (fb Lou Christie)**	**The Jury**	**1961**	**SN/ FG**
□○ **Little Beats**	**Someone For Me**	**1957**	**FC**
□○ **Little Eva & group**	**Locomotions**	**1962**	**FN/ FG**
□○ **Little Richard & group**	**True Fine Mama**	**1958**	**FC**
□○ **Little Sammy & group**	**Can You Love Me**	**1960**	**SC**
□○ Lollypops	Believe In Me	1958	FC
□○ **Loungers**	**Wedding Bells**	**1991**	**FC**

□○ **Loungers**	**Teenage Bells**	**1991**	**FC**
□○ **Love Larks**	**Diddle-Le-Bom**	**1957**	**FC**
□○ **Love Letters**	**Walking The Streets Alone**	**1957**	**SC**
□○ **Love-Lords**	**Burning Love**	**1962**	**SN**
□○ Love Notes (A)	Tonight	1957	FC
□○ Love Notes (A)	United	1957	SC
□○ **Love Notes (A)**	**If I Could Make You Mine**	**1957**	**SC**
□○ **Love Notes (A)**	**Don't Go**	**1957**	**FC**
□○ **Love Notes (B)**	**Dream Girl**	**1957**	**SC**
□○ **Lovetones**	**Talk To An Angel**	**1956**	**SC**
□○ Ly-Dells	Wizard Of Love	1961	FN
□○ **Ly-Dells**	**Teenage Tears**	**1961**	**FN**
□○ **Lydells**	**There Goes The Boy**	**1959**	**SN**
□○ **Lyrics**	**Oh Please Love Me**	**1959**	**SC**
□○ Lyrics	You And Your Fellow	1961	FN
□○ Lytations	Look Into The Sky	1964	FC
□○ Maestro, Johnny (& group)	What A Surprise	1961	SC
□○ Magnificent Four	The Closer You Are	1961	FN

□ ○ **Magnificent Four**	**Uncle Sam**	**1961**	**SN**
□ ○ Magnificents	Up On The Mountain	1956	FP
□ ○ Magnificents	Don't Leave Me	1958	FC
□ ○ Majestics (A)	Nitey Nite	1956	SC
□ ○ **Majestics (B)**	**Sweet One**	**1959**	**SC**
□ ○ **Majestics (B)**	**Searching For A New Love**	**1961**	**FN**
□ ○ Majors (A)	Laughing On The Outside, Crying On The Inside	1951	SP
□ ○ Majors (B)	A Wonderful Dream	1962	FN
□ ○ **Majors (B)**	**Tra La La**	**1963**	**FN**
□ ○ **Manhattan Transfer**	**Baby Come Back To Me**	**1984**	**FN**
□ ○ **Manhattan Transfer**	**That's The Way It Goes**	**1984**	**SN**
□ ○ **Manhattans, Eli Price & the**	**My Big Dream**	**1959**	**SC**
□ ○ Marcels	Blue Moon	1961	FN
□ ○ Marcels	Goodbye To Love	1961	SN
□ ○ Marcels	Heartaches	1961	FN
□ ○ **Marcels**	**Zoom**	**1961**	**FN**
□ ○ **Marcels**	**Summertime**	**1961**	**FN**

119

□○ **Marcels**	**Peace Of Mind**	**1961**	**SC**
□○ **Marcels**	**Sunday Kind Of Love**	**1961**	**SC**
□○ **Marcels**	**Crazy Bells In My Heart**	**1974**	**FN**
□○ **Marigolds**	**Rollin' Stone**	**1955**	**FC**
□○ **Marquis (A)**	**The Rain**	**1955**	**SC**
□○ **Marquis (A)**	**The Bells**	**1955**	**SC**
□○ Marquis (B)	Bohemian Daddy	1956	FC /FL
□○ Marvelettes	Please Mr. Postman	1961	FN /FG
□○ Marvelettes	Forever	1963	SN /FG
□○ Marvelows	I Do	1965	FN
□○ Marvels (aka Dubs)	I Won't Have You Breaking My Heart	1956	SC
□○ Marylanders	I'm A Sentimental Fool	1952	SP
□○ Marylanders	Make Me Thrill Again	1952	SP
□○ Master-Tones	Tell Me	1954	SP
□○ **Masters, Rick & the**	**Let It Please Be You**	**1963**	**SC**
□○ Masters, Rick & the	I Don't Want Your Love	1963	FN

□○ **Masters, Rick** **To Each His Own** **& the (with Bobby Young)**		**1968**	**SC**
□○ Matadors	Vengeance (Will Be Mine)	1958	SC
□○ **Maye, Arthur** **Moonlight** **Lee (& group)**		**1989**	**SC**
□○ **Maye, Arthur** **Happy And In Love** **Lee (& group)**		**1989**	**FC**
□○ McFadden, Ruth (bb/Royaltones)	Two In Love	1956	SC /FL
□○ **Meadowlarks,** **Love Only You** **Don Julian & the**		**1954**	**FC**
□○ Meadowlarks, Don Julian & the	Always And Always	1955	SP
□○ Meadowlarks, Don Julian & the	Heaven And Paradise	1955	SC
□○ Meadowlarks, Don Julian & the	This Must Be Paradise	1955	SC
□○ Medallions, Vernon Green & the	Buick '59	1954	FP
□○ Medallions, Vernon Green & the	The Letter	1954	SP
□○ **Medallions,** **Dear Ann** **Vernon Green & the**		**1962**	**SC**
□○ Mello-Harps	Love Is A Vow	1955	SC
□○ **Mello-Harps**	**I Love Only You**	**1955**	**SC**

□○ **Mello-Harps**	**What Good Are My Dreams**	**1956**	**SC**
□○ Mello-Kings	Tonight Tonight	1957	SC
□○ Mello Kings	The Only Girl (I'll Ever Love)	1958	SC
□○ Mello-Moods	How Could You	1952	SP
□○ Mello-Moods	Where Are You? (Now That I Need You)	1952	SP
□○ **Mello Moods**	**I'm Lost**	**1953**	**SP**
□○ Mellows, Lillian Leach & the	How Sentimental Can I Be?	1954	SP /FL
□○ Mellows, Lillian Leach & the	Smoke From Your Cigarette	1955	SP /FL
□○ Mellows, Lillian Leach & the	Yesterday's Memories	1955	SP /FL
□○ Mellows, Lillian Leach & the	My Darling	1956	SP /FL
□○ Mellows, Lillian Leach & the	Moon Of Silver	1956	SP /FL
□○ **Mellows, Lillian Leach & the**	**When The Lights Go On Again**	**1956**	**SC /FL**
□○ **Mellows, Lillian Leach & the**	**Gonna Pick Your Teeth With An Ice Pick**	**1956**	**MC /FL**
□○ **Melo Gents**	**Baby Be Mine**	**1959**	**SC**
□○ **Metallics**	**Need Your Love**	**1962**	**SN**

☐○ **Metronomes**	**Dear Don**	**1957**	**SC**
☐○ Metronomes	I Love My Girl	1957	SC
☐○ Midnighters (aka Royals)	Work With Me Annie	1953	FP
☐○ Midnighters (aka Royals)	Sexy Ways	1954	FP
☐○ **Midnighters (aka Royals)**	**Annie Had A Baby**	**1954**	**FP**
☐○ Midnighters (aka Royals)	Partners For Life	1956	SC
☐○ **Mighty Jupiters**	**Hy Wocky Toomba**	**1958**	**FC**
☐○ **Minors, Yvonne Lee & the**	**Jerry**	**1957**	**SC /FL**
☐○ **Mint Juleps**	**Bells Of Love**	**1956**	**SC**
☐○ **Miracles (w/Smokey Robinson)**	**Bad Girl**	**1959**	**SC**
☐○ **Mon-Claires**	**Please Come Back**	**1962**	**SN**
☐○ Monarchs (A)	Always Be Faithful	1956	FC
☐○ Monarchs (A)	In My Younger Days	1956	FC
☐○ Monarchs (A)	Pretty Little Girl	1956	FC
☐○ **Monarchs (B)**	**'Til I Hear It From You**	**1963**	**SN**
☐○ **Mondellos, Alice Jean & the**	**100 Years From Today**	**1957**	**SC/ FL**

□ ○ Moniques	I'm With You All The Way	1963	FC
□ ○ **Monorays**	**My Guardian Angel**	**1959**	**FC**
□ ○ **Monotones**	**You Never Loved Me**	**1957**	**SC**
□ ○ Monotones	Book Of Love	1958	FC
□ ○ **Monotones**	**The Legend Of Sleepy Hollow**	**1958**	**FC**
□ ○ Montclairs	Give Me A Chance	1956	SC
□ ○ **Moonglows**	**I Just Can't Tell No Lies**	**1952**	**FP**
□ ○ Moonglows	Secret Love	1954	SP
□ ○ Moonglows	Sincerely	1954	SP
□ ○ **Moonglows**	**219 Train**	**1954**	**FP**
□ ○ Moonglows	In My Diary	1955	SP
□ ○ Moonglows	Most Of All	1955	SP
□ ○ Moonglows	Seesaw	1956	FP
□ ○ Moonglows	We Go Together	1956	SP
□ ○ Moonglows	When I'm With You	1956	SP
□ ○ **Moonglows**	**Over And Over Again**	**1956**	**FC**
□ ○ **Moonglows**	**I Knew From The Start**	**1956**	**SC**
□ ○ **Moonglows**	**Twelve Months Of The Year**	**1959**	**SC**
□ ○ Moonglows, Bobby Lester & the	Penny Arcade	1962	SP

□ ○ Moonglows, Bobby Lester & the	Ten Commandments Of Love	1958	SC
□ ○ **Mr. Lee (bb/Cherokees)**	**The Decision**	**1960**	**SC**
□ ○ **Mysterials**	**Abracadabra**	**1995?**	**FN**
□ ○ **Mysterials**	**Shambalaya**	**1995?**	**FN**
□ ○ **Mystery Quartette**	**Go Tell Your Troubles To Somebody Else**	**1950**	**FP**
□ ○ **Mystics (A) (as the Overons)**	**Why Do You Pretend**	**1958**	**SC**
□ ○ **Mystics (A) (as the Overons)**	**The Bells Are Ringing**	**1958**	**FC**
□ ○ Mystics (A)	Don't Take The Stars	1959	FC
□ ○ Mystics (A)	Hushabye	1959	MC
□ ○ Mystics (A)	So Tenderly	1959	MC
□ ○ Mystics (A)	All Through The Night	1960	SC
□ ○ Mystics (A)	White Cliffs Of Dover	1960	FC
□ ○ Mystics (A)	Darling I Know Now	1961	FN
□ ○ **Mystics (A)**	**Now That Summer Is Here**	**1982**	**FC**
□ ○ **Mystics (B)**	**Stars In The Sky**	**1962**	**FC**
□ ○ Native Boys	Strange Love	1956	FC

125

□○ **Native Boys**	**Oh Let Me Dream**	**1956**	**SC**
□○ **Naturals, Yolanda & the**	**My Memories Of You**	**1962**	**SC/ FL**
□○ Neons	Angel Face	1956	FC
□○ **Neons**	**Honey Bun**	**1959**	**FN**
□○ New Yorkers 5	Gloria, My Darling	1955	SC
□○ **Newports**	**If I Could Tonight**	**1961**	**SN**
□○ **No Names**	**Love**	**1964**	**SN**
□○ Nobles, Nicky & the	Poor Rock & Roll	1958	FC
□○ **Nobles, Nicky & the**	**School Bells**	**1958**	**FC**
□○ **Nobles, Nicky & the**	**Crime Don't Pay**	**1962**	**FC**
□○ **Nobletones**	**Dream Girl**	**1958**	**SC**
□○ **Nobletones**	**I Love You**	**1958**	**FC**
□○ Note-Torials	My Valerie	1959	FC
□○ Nutmegs	Ship Of Love	1955	SC
□○ Nutmegs	Story Untold	1955	SC
□○ Nutmegs	Whispering Sorrows	1955	SC
□○ Nutmegs	A Love So True	1956	SC
□○ **Nutmegs**	**Comin' Home**	**1956**	**FC**

□○ **Nutmegs**	**Key To The Kingdom (Of Your Heart)**	**1956**	**SC**
□○ **Nutmegs**	**I Fell In Love**	**1957**	**SC**
□○ Nutmegs	My Story	1959	SC
□○ Nutmegs	Down In Mexico	1963	FC
□○ Nutmegs	Down To Earth	1963	SC
□○ Nutmegs	Hello	1963	SC
□○ Nutmegs	Let Me Tell You	1963	FC
□○ **Nutmegs**	**The Way Love Should Be**	**1963**	**SC**
□○ **Nutmegs**	**You're Crying**	**1964**	**SC**
□○ **Ocapellos**	**The Stars**	**1966**	**SN**
□○ **Off Keys**	**Our Wedding Day**	**1962**	**SN**
□○ **Off Keys**	**Singing Bells**	**1962**	**FN**
□○ Olympics	Western Movies	1958	FC
□○ **Olympics**	**Big Boy Pete**	**1960**	**FC**
□○ Olympics	Dance By The Light Of The Moon	1960	FN
□○ Opals (aka Crystals)	Come To Me Darling	1954	SP
□○ Opals (aka Crystals)	My Heart's Desire	1954	SP

127

□○ Orchids	Newly Wed	1955	SC
□○ Orchids	You Said You Loved Me	1955	SC
□○ Orchids	You're Everything To Me	1955	SC
□○ **Orbits**	**Message Of Love**	**1956**	**SC**
□○ Orients	Queen Of The Angels	1964	SN
□○ **Orients**	**Shouldn't I**	**1964**	**FC**
□○ Orioles, Sonny Til & the	It's Too Soon To Know	1948	SP
□○ Orioles, Sonny Til & the	A Kiss And A Rose	1949	SP
□○ Orioles, Sonny Til & the	Tell Me So	1949	SP
□○ Orioles, Sonny Til & the	What Are You Doing New	1949	SP
□○ Orioles, Sonny Til & the	At Night	1950	SP
□○ Orioles,Sonny Til & the	I'd Rather Have You Under The Moon	1950	SP
□○ **Orioles, Sonny Til & the**	**Would You Still Be The One In My Heart**	**1950**	**SP**
□○ **Orioles, Sonny Til & the**	**Moonlight**	**1950**	**SP**
□○ Orioles, Sonny Til & the	I Miss You So	1951	SP
□○ Orioles, Sonny Til & the	Crying In The Chapel	1953	SP

□○ Orioles, Sonny Til & the	I Cover The Waterfront	1953	SP
□○ **Orioles, Sonny Til & the**	**In The Chapel In The Moonlight**	**1954**	**SP**
□○ **Orioles, Sonny Til & the**	**For All We Know**	**1956**	**SP**
□○ **Orlando, Tony (& group)**	**Ding Dong**	**1959**	**FC**
□○ **Orlandos**	**Cloudburst**	**1957**	**SC**
□○ **Orlons**	**Heart Darling Angel**	**1961**	**SN /FL**
□○ **Orlons**	**Happy Birthday, Mr. 21**	**1962**	**SN /FL**
□○ **Ovations**	**The Day We Fell In Love**	**1961**	**SN**
□○ Oxfords, Darrell & the	Picture In My Wallet	1959	SN
□○ Packards	Dream Of Love	1956	SC
□○ **Pals**	**Summer Is Here**	**1959**	**SC**
□○ Paradons	Diamonds And Pearls	1960	SN
□○ **Paradons**	**I Had A Dream**	**1961**	**SC**
□○ Paragons	Florence	1957	SC
□○ Paragons	Hey, Little School Girl	1957	FC
□○ Paragons	Let's Start All Over Again	1957	SC

□ ○ Paragons	Stick With Me Baby	1957	FC
□ ○ Paragons	So You Will Know	1958	SC
□ ○ Paragons	The Vows Of Love	1958	SC
□ ○ Paragons	Twilight	1958	SC
□ ○ **Paragons**	**If**	**1961**	**SC**
□ ○ Passions	Just To Be With You	1959	SC
□ ○ Passions	I Only Want You	1960	FC
□ ○ Passions	This Is My Love	1960	SC
□ ○ **Passions**	**Gloria**	**1960**	**SN**
□ ○ **Passions**	**Made For Lovers**	**1960**	**FN**
□ ○ Pastels	Been So Long	1958	SP
□ ○ Pastels	So Far Away	1958	SP
□ ○ Pearls	Let's You And I Go Steady	1956	FC
□ ○ **Pearls**	**Zippity Zippity Zoom**	**1956**	**FC**
□ ○ **Pearls**	**I Sure Need You**	**1957**	**FC**
□ ○ Pearls	Your Cheating Heart	1957	FC
□ ○ **Pelicans**	**Chimes**	**1954**	**SP**
□ ○ **Pelicans**	**Aurelia**	**1954**	**SP**
□ ○ Penguins	Earth Angel	1954	SP
□ ○ Penguins	Hey Senorita	1954	FP

□ ○ **Penguins**	**Love Will Make Your Mind Go Wild**	**1955**	**SC**
□ ○ **Penguins**	**Ookey-Ook**	**1955**	**FC**
□ ○ Penguins	My Troubles Are Not At End	1956	SC
□ ○ Penguins	Memories Of El Monte	1963	SN
□ ○ Pentagons	To Be Loved (Forever)	1960	SN
□ ○ **Pentagons**	**Until Then**	**1962**	**FN**
□ ○ Perfections	Hey Girl	1959	FC
□ ○ **Perfections**	**(The Girl With The) Crimson Hair**	**1962**	**FN**
□ ○ Personalities	Woe Woe Baby	1957	FC
□ ○ Personalities	Yours To Command	1957	SC
□ ○ **Personalities**	**Little Girl I Want You**	**1957**	**FC**
□ ○ **Phantoms**	**Shoobie Doobie Mama**	**1956**	**FC**
□ ○ **Pharaohs, Richard Berry & the**	**Take The Key (And Open Up My Heart)**	**1956**	**SC**
□ ○ **Pharaohs, Richard Berry & the**	**Louie Louie**	**1957**	**FC**
□ ○ **Pharaohs, Richard Berry & the**	**Have Love Will Travel**	**1959**	**FC**
□ ○ Phillips, Phil (w/ Twilights)	Sea Of Love	1959	SN
□ ○ **Pipes**	**Be Fair**	**1956**	**SC**

131

☐○ Pips	Every Beat Of My Heart	1961	SC /FL
☐○ Pixies Three	442 Glenwood Avenue 1	1963	FN /FG
☐○ Pixies Three	Birthday Party	1963	FN /FG
☐○ **Plaids**	**Hungry For Your Love**	**1958**	**SC**
☐○ **Planetones, Kenny Vance & the**	**Looking For An Echo**	**1975**	**SN**
☐○ **Planetones, Kenny Vance & the**	**The Way You Look Tonight**	**2004?**	**SN**
☐○ **Planetones, Kenny Vance & the**	**Diamonds And Pearls**	**2004?**	**SN**
☐○ **Planetones, Kenny Vance & the**	**For Your Precious Love**	**2004?**	**SN**
☐○ **Planetones, Kenny Vance & the**	**What Are You Doing**	**2004?**	**SN**
☐○ **Planetones, Kenny Vance & the**	**Hey Señorita**	**2004?**	**FN**
☐○ Plants	Dear I Swear	1957	FC
☐○ **Plants**	**It's You**	**1957**	**SC**
☐○ Platters	I'll Cry When You're Gone	1953	SP
☐○ **Platters**	**Give Thanks**	**1953**	**SP**
☐○ Platters	Voo-Vee-Ah-Bee	1954	FP

□○ Platters	Only You (And You Alone)	1955	SP
□○ Platters	The Great Pretender	1955	SP
□○ **Platters**	**Glory Of Love**	**1955**	**SC**
□○ Platters	Heaven On Earth	1956	SP
□○ Platters	My Prayer	1956	SP
□○ Platters	On My Word Of Honor	1956	SP
□○ Platters	You'll Never Never Know	1956	SP
□○ Platters	(You've Got) The Magic Touch	1956	SP
□○ Platters	My Dream	1957	SP
□○ **Platters**	**I'm Sorry**	**1957**	**SP**
□○ **Platters**	**He's Mine**	**1957**	**FC/ FL**
□○ Platters	Smoke Gets In Your Eyes	1958	SP
□○ Platters	Twilight Time	1958	SP
□○ Platters	Harbor Lights	1960	SP
□○ **Poets**	**Vowels Of Love**	**1958**	**FC**
□○ Poni-Tails	Born Too Late	1958	SC /FG
□○ **Preludes**	**Kingdom Of Love**	**1958**	**FC**
□○ **Preludes 5**	**Starlight**	**1961**	**FN**
□○ **Preludes 5**	**Don't You Know**	**1961**	**SC**

133

□○ Premiers (A)	My Darling	1956	SC
□○ Premiers (A)	Is This A Dream?	1957	SC
□○ Premiers (B)	Help	1960	FC
□○ **Premonitions**	**My Girl Pearl**	**1967**	**FN**
□○ **Pretenders (w/Jimmy Jones)**	**I've Got To Have You, Baby**	**1956**	**FC**
□○ **Pretenders**	**Smile**	**1961**	**SN**
□○ **Princetones**	**Bada Bada**	**1958**	**FC**
□○ Prisonaires	Just Walkin' In The Rain	1953	SP
□○ **Prodigals**	**Marsha**	**1958**	**FC**
□○ Pyramids (A)	And I Need You	1955	SC
□○ Pyramids (B)	Ankle Bracelet	1958	SC
□○ Pyramids (B)	Hot Dog Dooly Wah	1958	FC
□○ Queens (Shirley Gunter & the)	Oop-Shoop	1954	FP /FG
□○ Queens (Shirley Gunter & the)	You're Mine	1955	FP /FG
□○ **Question (?) Marks**	**Another Soldier Gone**	**1954**	**SP**
□○ Quin-Tones	Down The Aisle Of Love	1958	SC /FG
□○ **Quin-Tones**	**There'll Be No Sorrow**	**1958**	**SC FG**

□○ **Quintones** (aka Quin-Tones)	**Ding Dong**	**1958**	**SC /FG**
□○ Quinns	Hong Kong	1958	FC
□○ Quinns	Oh Starlight	1958	SC
□○ **Quinns**	**Unfaithful**	**1965**	**SN**
□○ Quotations	Ala-Men-Sa-Aye	1961	FN
□○ Quotations	Imagination	1961	FN
□○ **Quotations**	**Time Was**	**1959**	**SN**
□○ **Radiants**	**Ra Cha Cha**	**1959**	**FC**
□○ Rainbows (A)	Mary Lee	1955	FC
□○ Rainbows (A)	Stay	1956	SC
□○ **Rainbows (A)**	**Shirley**	**1956**	**FC**
□○ Rainbows (A)	They Say	1957	SC
□○ Rainbows (B), Randy & the	Denise	1963	FN
□○ Rainbows (B). Randy & the	She's My Angel	1963	FC
□○ **Rainbows (B), Randy & the**	**Why Do Kids Grow Up**	**1963**	**FN**
□○ **Rainbows (B), Randy & the**	**Debbie**	**1982**	**FN**
□○ Raindrops (A)	(I Found) Heaven In Love	1956	SC

135

☐○ Raindrops (B)	The Kind Of Boy You Can't Forget	1963	FN /FL
☐○ **Raindrops (B)**	**What A Guy**	**1963**	**FC /FL**
☐○ Rajahs (aka Nutmegs)	Shifting Sands	1957	FC
☐○ Ramblers (A)	Vadunt-Un-Va-Da Song	1954	SP
☐○ Ramblers (B)	Come On Back	1963	FC
☐○ **Ramblers (B)**	**So Sad**	**1963**	**MC**
☐○ Ravels, Sheriff & the	Shombalor	1959	FC
☐○ Ravens	Lullabye	1946	SP
☐○ **Ravens**	**My Sugar Is So Refined**	**1946**	**FP**
☐○ **Ravens**	**Bye Bye Baby Blues**	**1946**	**FP**
☐○ Ravens	Once In A While	1948	SP
☐○ Ravens	September Song	1948	SP
☐○ Ravens	Until The Real Thing Comes Along	1948	SP
☐○ Ravens	Count Every Star	1950	SP
☐○ Ravens	Time Takes Care Of Everything	1950	SP
☐○ Ravens	You Foolish thing	1951	SP
☐○ **Ravens (w/Dinah Washington)**	**Out In The Cold Again**	**1951**	**SP**
☐○ Ravens	Don't Mention My Name	1953	SP

□○ **Ravens**	**Green Eyes**	**1955**	**FP**
□○ **Ravons**	**Everybody's Laughing At Me**	**1962**	**SN/ FL**
□○ Rays	Silhouettes	1957	SC
□○ **Rays**	**Triangle**	**1958**	**SC**
□○ **Re-Vels**	**Love My Baby**	**1954**	**FC**
□○ **Re-Vels**	**You Lied To Me**	**1955**	**SC**
□○ **Re-Vels**	**So In Love**	**1956**	**SC**
□○ Re-Vels	False Alarm	1958	FC
□○ **Reflections**	**I Really Must Must Know**	**1961**	**FN**
□○ **Reflections**	**Rocket To The Moon**	**1962**	**FN**
□○ Reflections	(Just Like) Romeo And Juliet	1964	FN
□○ Regan, Tommy (bb/Marcels)	I'll Never Stop Loving You	1964	FN
□○ Regents	Barbara Ann	1961	FN
□○ Regents	Runaround	1961	FN
□○ **Regents**	**Liar**	**1961**	**FN**
□○ **Relatives, Ronnie & the**	**I Want A Boy**	**1961**	**FN/ FG**
□○ **Reno, Al (w/Dials)**	**Cheryl**	**1961**	**FN**

□○ **Reunion**	**Wonderful Tonight**	**1987**	**SC**
□○ Revalons	Dreams Are For Fools	1958	FC
□○ **Revels**	**Dead Man's Stroll**	**1959**	**SC**
□○ **Rhythm Cadets**	**Dearest Doryce**	**1957**	**SC**
□○ Rialtos	Let Me In	1962	FN
□○ Riffs	Little Girl	1964	FN
□○ **Rivals**	**Riggety Tick**	**1957**	**FC**
□○ Rivera, Lucy (& group)	Make Me Queen Again	1959	SN /FL
□○ Rivieras	Count Every Star	1958	SN
□○ Rivieras	Moonlight Cocktails	1960	SC
□○ Rivileers	A Thousand Stars	1954	SP
□○ Rivingtons	Papa Oom-Mow-Mow	1962	FN
□○ Rob Roys, Norman Fox & the	Tell Me Why	1957	FC
□○ **Rob-Roys, Norman Fox & the**	**Audrey**	**1957**	**SC**
□○ Rob Roys, Norman Fox & the	Dance Girl Dance	1958	FC
□○ **Rob-Roys, Norman Fox & the**	**My Dearest One**	**1958**	**SC**
□○ Rob Roys, Norman Fox & the	Dream Girl	1958	FC
□○ Rob Roys,	Pizza Pie	1958	FC

Norman Fox & the

□○ Rob Roys, Norman Fox & the	Lover Doll	1972	FC
□○ **Rob-Roys,** **Norman Fox & the**	**That's Love**	**1988**	**FC**
□○ **Rob-Roys,** **Norman Fox & the**	**Do-Re-Mi**	**1990**	**FC**
□○ **Robins** **(w/Little Esther)**	**Double Crossin' Blues**	**1950**	**SP/** **FL**
□○ Robins	A Fool Such As I	1952	SP
□○ Robins	How Would You Know	1953	SP
□○ Robins	Smoky Joe's Cafe	1955	FP
□○ **Rocka-Fellas**	**Strike It Rich**	**1963**	**FN**
□○ **Rocketeers**	**My Reckless Heart**	**1958**	**SC**
□○ Rocketones	Dee I	1957	SC
□○ Rocketones	Mexico	1957	FC
□○ Rockin' Chairs, Lenny Dean & the	A Kiss Is A Kiss	1959	FC
□○ Rockin' Chairs , Lenny Dean & the	Memories Of Love	1959	FC
□○ Rockin' Chairs, Lenny Dean & the	Please Mary Lou	1959	FC
□○ **Rockin Dukes**	**Angel And A Rose**	**1957**	**SC**
□○ **Rocky Fellers**	**Killer Joe**	**1963**	**FN**

□○ **Romancers**	**I Still Remember**	**1956**	**SC**
□○ Romans (Little Caesar & the)	Those Oldies But Goodies (Remind Me Of You)	1961	SN
□○ Roomates (A)	Band Of Gold	1961	SN
□○ Roomates (A) Cathy Jean & the	Please Love Me Forever	1960	SN /FL
□○ **Roomates (A)**	**Glory Of Love**	**1961**	**SC**
□○ **Roomates (A)**	**Sunday Kind Of Love**	**1962**	**SC**
□○ **Roomates (B)**	**Alemensay**	**2013**	**FC**
□○ **Roomates (B)**	**Childish Ways**	**2013**	**FC**
□○ **Roomates (B)**	**Little Miss America**	**2013**	**FC**
□○ Rosebuds	Dearest Darling	1957	SC /FG
□○ Roulettes	I See A Star	1958	SC
□○ **Royal Holidays**	**Down In Cuba**	**1959**	**FC**
□○ **Royal Jesters**	**Love Me**	**1961**	**SC**
□○ **Royal Teens**	**Short Shorts**	**1957**	**FC**
□○ Royal Teens	Believe Me	1959	FC
□○ Royals (A), (aka Midnighters)	A Love Of My Heart	1952	SP
□○ Royals (A), (aka Midnighters)	Every Beat Of My Heart	1952	SP

□○ Royals (A), (aka Midnighters)	Moonrise	1952	SP
□○ Royals (A), (aka Midnighters)	Starting From Tonight	1952	SP
□○ Royals (B), Richie & the	And When I'm Near You	1961	FN
□○ **Royals (B), Richie & the**	**Be My Girl**	**1962**	**FN**
□○ **Royals (B), Richie & the**	**I Only Want You**	**1963**	**FC**
□○ Royaltones	Crazy Love	1956	FC
□○ **Royaltones**	**Hong Kong Jelly Wong**	**1956**	**FN**
□○ **Royaltones**	**Never Let Me Go**	**1956**	**SC**
□○ Safaris	Image Of A Girl	1960	SC
□○ **Safaris**	**Four Steps To Love**	**1960**	**FC**
□○ **Saigons**	**You're Heavenly**	**1955**	**SC**
□○ **Salutations, Vito & the**	**Your Way**	**1962**	**SC**
□○ **Salutations, Vito & the**	**Gloria**	**1962**	**SC**
□○ Salutations, Vito & the	Unchained Melody	1963	FN
□○ **Saunders, Little Butchie & group**	**Don't Do Me Wrong**	**1956**	**SC**

141

□ ○ **Savoys (A),** James (Jimmy) Jones & the	**Say You're Mine**	**1956**	**FC**
□ ○ **Savoys (B)**	**Gloria**	**1965**	**SC**
□ ○ **Savoys (B)**	**Closer You Are**	**1965**	**FC**
□ ○ Scarlets	Dear One	1954	SP
□ ○ Scarlets	Love Doll	1955	SC
□ ○ **Scarlets**	**True Love**	**1955**	**SC**
□ ○ **Scarlets,** Fred Parris & the	**She's Gone (With The Wind)**	**1958**	**SC**
□ ○ Schoolboys	Please Say You Want Me	1957	SC
□ ○ Schoolboys	Shirley	1957	FC
□ ○ **Schoolboys**	**Ding A Ling Coo Coo Mop**	**1957**	**FC**
□ ○ **Schoolboys**	**I Am Old Enough**	**1957**	**SC**
□ ○ Schoolboys	Angel Of Love	1958	SC
□ ○ Scott Brothers	Part Of You	1959	FC
□ ○ Selections	Guardian Angel	1958	FC
□ ○ **Selections**	**Soft And Sweet**	**1958**	**SC**
□ ○ Senors	May I Have This Dance	1962	MN
□ ○ Sensations	Please Mr. Disc Jockey	1956	SP /FL
□ ○ **Sensations**	**Yes Sir, That's My Baby**	**1956**	**SC /FL**

☐○ Sensations	My Debut To Love	1957	SP /FL
☐○ Sensations	Let Me In	1961	FN /FL
☐○ **Sensations**	**Music, Music, Music**	**1961**	**FC /FL**
☐○ **Sentimentals**	**Sunday Kind Of Love**	**1957**	**FC**
☐○ Serenaders	I Wrote A Letter	1957	FC
☐○ **Serenaders**	**Never Let Me Go**	**1957**	**SC**
☐○ **Shallows**	**On The Sunny Side Of The Street**	**1986**	**FC**
☐○ **Sharks Quintet**	**The Glory Of Love**	**1974**	**SP**
☐○ **Sharmeers**	**A Schoolgirl In Love**	**1958**	**SC /FG**
☐○ Sharps	Love Me My Darling	1954	SP
☐○ **Sharps**	**Six Months Three Weeks Two Day & An Hour**	**1957**	**SC**
☐○ **Sheiks**	**Sentimental Heart**	**1955**	**SC**
☐○ **Sheiks**	**Give Me Another Chance**	**1955**	**SC**
☐○ Shells	Baby Oh Baby	1957	SC
☐○ Shells	What's In An Angel's Eyes	1957	SC
☐○ Shells	Sippin' Soda	1958	SC

□○ **Shells**	**Pleading No More**	**1958**	**FC**
□○ **Shells**	**Explain It To Me**	**1961**	**SC**
□○ **Shells**	**Deep In My Heart**	**1962**	**SC**
□○ **Shells**	**(It's A) Happy Holiday**	**1962**	**FC**
□○ Shepherd Sisters	Alone	1957	FC /FG
□○ Sheppards	Sherry	1956	SC
□○ Sheppards	Island Of Love	1959	SC
□○ **Sheppards**	**Queen Of Hearts**	**1961**	**SN**
□○ **Sheps**	**Untrue**	**1993**	**SC**
□○ **Sheps**	**Tormented**	**1993**	**SC**
□○ **Sheps**	**Heaven Above Me**	**1993**	**FC**
□○ **Sheps**	**Where Are You**	**1993**	**SC**
□○ **Sheps**	**Be Fair**	**1995**	**SC**
□○ **Sherwoods**	**Love You Madly**	**1967**	**FC /FG**
□○ Shields	You Cheated	1958	SC
□○ Shirelles	I Met Him On A Sunday	1958	FC /FG
□○ **Shirelles**	**I Want You To Be My Boyfriend**	**1958**	**SC /FG**

□○ Shirelles	Dedicated To The One I Love	1959	SN /FG
□○ Shirelles	Tonight's The Night	1960	MN /FG
□○ Shirelles	Will You Love Me Tomorrow	1960	MN /FG
□○ **Shirelles**	**Boys**	**1960**	**FN /FG**
□○ **Shirelles**	**What A Sweet Thing That Was**	**1961**	**FN /FG**
□○ Shirelles	Baby It's You	1961	SN /FG
□○ Shirelles	Mama Said	1961	FN /FG
□○ Shirelles	Soldier Boy	1962	SN /FG
□○ **Shirelles**	**Everybody Loves A Lover**	**1962**	**FN /FG**
□○ **Shirelles**	**Foolish Little Girl**	**1963**	**MN /FG**
□○ Showmen	It Will Stand	1961	FN
□○ **Shy-Tones**	**A Lover's Quarrel**	**1960**	**SN**
□○ Silhouettes	Get A Job	1957	FC
□○ Silhouettes	Bing Bong	1958	FC
□○ Silhouettes	I Sold My Heart To The Junkman	1958	SC

145

☐○ **Silva-Tones**	**That's All I Want From You (Chi-Wah-Wah)**	**1956**	**FC**
☐○ **Sinceres**	**Do You Remember**	**1960**	**SC**
☐○ Sinceres	Please Don't Cheat On Me	1961	FN
☐○ Six Teens	A Casual Look	1956	SC /FL
☐○ Skarlettones	Do You Remember	1959	FC
☐○ Skyliners	It Happened Today	1959	FC
☐○ Skyliners	Lonely Way	1959	FC
☐○ Skyliners	Since I Don't Have You	1959	SN
☐○ Skyliners	This I Swear	1959	SN
☐○ Skyliners	Pennies From Heaven	1960	FC
☐○ **Slades**	**You Cheated**	**1958**	**SC**
☐○ **Smith, Huey & group**	**Dearest Darling (You're The One)**	**1959**	**SC**
☐○ **Socialites, Kenny & the**	**I'll Have To Decide**	**1958**	**SC**
☐○ Solitaires	Blue Valentine	1954	SC
☐○ Solitaires	Please Remember My Heart	1954	SC
☐○ Solitaires	South Of The Border	1954	MC
☐○ Solitaires	Wonder Why	1954	SC
☐○ Solitaires	I Don't Stand A Ghost Of A Chance	1955	SC

□○ Solitaires	Later For You Baby	1955	FC
□○ **Solitaires**	**What Did She Say**	**1955**	**FC**
□○ Solitaires	Nothing Like A Little Love	1956	SC
□○ Solitaires	The Angels Sang	1956	SC
□○ Solitaires	You've Sinned	1956	SC
□○ **Solitaires**	**Magic Rose**	**1956**	**SC**
□○ **Solitaires**	**Come Back And Give Me Your Hand**	**1956**	**SC**
□○ Solitaires	I Really Love You So (Honey Babe)	1957	FC
□○ Solitaires	Walkin' Along	1957	FC
□○ **Sonics**	**This Broken Heart**	**1959**	**SC**
□○ **Sonnets**	**Why Should We Break Up**	**1956**	**FC**
□○ **Sophomores, Anthony & the**	**Gee (But I'd Give The World)**	**1959**	**SC**
□○ **Sophomores, Anthony & the**	**Don't Play That Song**	**1963**	**FN**
□○ Sophomores, Anthony & the	Embraceable You	1963	SC
□○ Sophomores, Anthony & the	Play Those Oldies Mr. D.J.	1963	FN
□○ Souvenirs	Double Dealing Baby	1957	FP
□○ Spaniels	Baby It's You	1953	SP

147

□○ Spaniels	The Bells Ring Out	1953	SP
□○ Spaniels	Goodnite Sweetheart Goodnite	1953	SP
□○ Spaniels	Let's Make Up	1954	SC
□○ Spaniels	You Painted Pictures	1955	SC
□○ Spaniels	You Gave Me Peace Of Mind	1956	SC
□○ Spaniels	Everyone's Laughing	1957	MC
□○ **Spaniels**	**I Lost You**	**1957**	**SC**
□○ **Spaniels**	**Here Is Why I Love You**	**1957**	**SC**
□○ **Spaniels**	**This Is A Lovely Way To Spend An Evening**	**1958**	**SC**
□○ Spaniels	Stormy Weather	1958	FC
□○ **Spaniels**	**One Hundred Years From Today**	**1959**	**SC**
□○ **Spaniels**	**These Three Words**	**1959**	**SC**
□○ **Spaniels**	**People Will Say We're In Love**	**1959**	**FC**
□○ **Spaniels**	**I Know, I Know**	**1960**	**SC**
□○ Spectors Three	I Really Do	1960	MN
□○ **Spidells**	**Come Walk With Me**	**1960**	**SC**
□○ Spiders	I Didn't Want To Do It	1954	FP
□○ Spiders	I'm Slippin' In	1954	FP

□○ Spiders	Love's All I'm Puttin' Down (rel. 1992)	1954	FP
□○ Spiders	Witchcraft	1955	FP
□○ **Spiders**	**Bells In My Heart**	**1955**	**SP**
□○ Spiders	That's My Desire	1957	SP
□○ **Spinners (A)**	**My Love And Your Love**	**1958**	**SC**
□○ Spinners (B), Claudine Clark & the	Party Lights	1962	FN /FL
□○ **Squires**	**Heavenly Angel**	**1955**	**SC**
□○ **Squires**	**Sindy**	**1955**	**SC**
□○ Squires	Dreamy Eyes	1957	SC
□○ Starlites	Missing You	1957	SC
□○ **Starlarks**	**Fountain Of Love**	**1957**	**SC**
□○ **Starlighters**	**A Story Of Love**	**1960**	**MC**
□○ **Starlings**	**My Plea For Love**	**1954**	**SP**
□○ **Starliters, Joey Dee & the**	**Lorraine**	**1958**	**SC**
□○ Starlites. Eddie & the	To Make A Long Story Short	1959	SC
□○ Starlites, Eddie & the	Come On Home	1963	SN
□○ Starlites, Jackie & the	Valerie	1960	SC

☐○ **Starlites**	**Way Up In The Sky**	**1960**	**FC**
☐○ **Stereos**	**A Love For Only You**	**1959**	**SC**
☐○ Stereos	I Really Love You	1961	FN
☐○ **Storytellers**	**You Played Me A Fool**	**1959**	**SC**
☐○ **Storytellers**	**Please Remember My Love**	**1989**	**SC**
☐○ **Storytellers**	**Heaven's For Real**	**1989**	**SC**
☐○ Strangers	Blue Flowers	1954	SP
☐○ Strangers	Hoping You'll Understand	1954	SP
☐○ Strangers	My Friends	1954	SP
☐○ **Street-Tones, Patty & the**	**Rendezvous With You**	**1979**	**FC**
☐○ **Street-Tones, Patty & the**	**I'm So In Love**	**1979**	**SC**
☐○ **Street-Tones, Patty & the**	**Let It Please Be You**	**1980**	**SC**
☐○ **Students**	**Bye Bye Truly**	**1957**	**FC**
☐○ Students	Every Day Of The Week	1958	FC
☐○ Students	I'm So Young	1958	SC
☐○ **Students**	**My Vow To You**	**1958**	**SC**
☐○ **Students**	**Mommy And Daddy**	**1958**	**FC**

□ ○ **Suburbans**	**Alphabet Of Love**	**1959**	**FC**
□ ○ **Suddens** (aka Safaris)	**Childish Ways**	**1961**	**FN**
□ ○ **Sultans**	**It'll Be Easy**	**1961**	**SC**
□ ○ Summits	Go Back Where You Came Come	1961	FN
□ ○ **Sunbeams**	**Tell Me Why**	**1955**	**SC**
□ ○ Sunbeams	Please Say You'll Be Mine	1957	SC
□ ○ Superiors	Lost Love	1957	SC
□ ○ **Superiors**	**Don't Say Goodbye**	**1957**	**FC**
□ ○ Supremes (A)	Could This Be You	1956	SP
□ ○ Supremes (B), Ruth McFadden & the	Darling, Listen To The Words Of This Song	1956	SP /FL
□ ○ Supremes (C)	Just For You And I	1957	SC
□ ○ **Supremes (C)**	**Honey Honey**	**1957**	**FC**
□ ○ Swallows	Dearest	1951	SP
□ ○ Swallows	Eternally	1951	SP
□ ○ Swallows	It Ain't The Meat	1951	FP
□ ○ Swallows	Since You've Been Away	1951	SP
□ ○ Swallows	Will You Be Mine	1951	SP
□ ○ Swallows	Beside You	1952	SP
□ ○ **Swallows**	**I Only Have Eyes For You**	**1952**	**SP**

151

□ ○ Swallows	Please Baby Please	1952	MP
□ ○ Swans	My True Love	1953	SP
□ ○ **Sweet Teens, Faith Taylor & the**	**I Need Him To Love Me**	**1959**	**SC/ FG**
□ ○ Swinging Hearts	How Can I Love You	1961	SN
□ ○ **Swinging Hearts**	**Please Say It Isn't So**	**1964**	**SN**
□ ○ **Tamerlanes, Barry & the**	**I Wonder What She's Doing Tonight**	**1963**	**FN**
□ ○ Teardrops	The Stars Are Out Tonight	1954	SC
□ ○ **Tears, Linda & the**	**Good Goodbye**	**1965**	**SC/ FL**
□ ○ Techniques	Hey! Little Girl	1957	SC
□ ○ Teddy Bears	To Know Him Is To Love Him	1957	SC /FL
□ ○ Teenagers, Frankie Lymon & the	ABCs Of Love	1956	FC
□ ○ Teenagers, Frankie Lymon & the	I Promise To Remember	1956	FC
□ ○ Teenagers, Frankie Lymon & the	I Want You To Be My Girl	1956	FC
□ ○ Teenagers, Frankie Lymon & the	I'm Not A Know It All	1956	SC
□ ○ Teenagers, Frankie Lymon & the	Share	1956	SC

☐○ Teenagers, Frankie Lymon & the	Why Do Fools Fall In Love	1956	FC
☐○ **Teenagers, Frankie Lymon & the**	**Please Be Mine**	**1956**	**SC**
☐○ **Teenagers, Frankie Lymon & the**	**Who Can Explain**	**1956**	**FC**
☐○ **Teenagers, Frankie Lymon & the**	**I'm Not A Juvenile Delinquent**	**1956**	**FC**
☐○ **Teenagers, Frankie Lymon & the**	**Baby Baby**	**1956**	**FC**
☐○ Teenagers, Frankie Lymon & the	Out In The Cold Again	1957	SC
☐○ Teenagers, Frankie Lymon & the	Paper Castles	1957	FC
☐○ Teenagers, Frankie Lymon & the	Teenage Love	1957	FC
☐○ **Teenagers, Frankie Lymon & the**	**Creation Of Love**	**1957**	**SC**
☐○ Teenchords, Lewis Lymon & the	Honey Honey	1957	FC
☐○ Teenchords, Lewis Lymon & the	I'm Not Too Young To Fall In Love	1957	FC
☐○ Teenchords, Lewis Lymon & the	I'm So Happy (Tra-La-La-La)	1957	FC
☐○ Teenchords, Lewis Lymon & the	Please Tell The Angels	1957	SC

□○ Teenchords, Lewis Lymon & the	Your Last Chance	1957	FC
□○ **Teenchords, Lewis Lymon & the**	**Too Young**	**1957**	**FC**
□○ **Teenchords, Lewis Lymon & the**	**Dance Girl**	**1958**	**FC**
□○ **Teenchords, Lewis Lymon & the**	**Them There Eyes**	**1958**	**FC**
□○ Tempo-Tones, Nancy Lee &	So They Say	1957	SC /FL
□○ Tempo-Tones (w/Richard Lanham)	Get Yourself Another Fool	1957	SC
□○ **Temptations (A)**	**Roaches Rock**	**1958**	**FC**
□○ Temptations (A)	Standing Alone	1958	FC
□○ Temptations (B)	Barbara	1960	FC
□○ **Terracetones (aka Monotones)**	**Ride Of Paul Revere**	**1958**	**FC**
□○ **Thrashers**	**Jeannie**	**1957**	**FC**
□○ Three Chuckles (w/Teddy Randazzo)	Runaround	1954	SP
□○ Three Chuckles	Foolishly	1955	SP
□○ Three Friends	Blanche	1956	SC
□○ **Thrillers (A)**	**'Lizabeth**	**1954**	**FP**
□○ Thrillers (B), Little Joe & the	Peanuts	1957	FC

□○ **Tigers, Little**	**Lonely, Lonely Nights**	**1957**	**SC**
Julian Herrera & the			
□○ **Tigers, Little**	**I Remember Linda**	**1957**	**SC**
Julian Herrera & the			
□○ Timetones	I've Got A Feeling	1961	SN
(aka Time-Tones)			
□○ Timetones	In My Heart	1961	FC
(aka Time-Tones)			
□○ Timetones	Pretty Pretty Girl (The New	1961	FC
(aka Time-Tones)	Beat)		
□○ **Timetones**	**My Love**	**1961**	**SN**
(aka Time-Tones)			
□○ **Timetones**	**House Where Lovers**	**1963**	**FN**
(aka Time-Tones)	**Dream**		
□○ **Timetones**	**Sunday Kind Of Love**	**1964**	**FC**
(aka Time-Tones)			
□○ Tokens (A)	Doom Lang	1957	FC
□○ **Tokens (A)**	**Come Dance With Me**	**1957**	**FC**
□○ **Tokens (B)**	**While I Dream**	**1958**	**FC**
(w/Neil Sedaka)			
□○ Tokens (B)	Tonight I Fell In Love	1961	FN
□○ **Tokens (B)**	**Tina**	**1961**	**FN**
□○ Tokens (B)	The Lion Sleeps Tonight	1961	MN
□○ **Tokens (B)**	**Portrait Of My Love**	**1967**	**FN**

□ ○ Tonettes	Oh What A Baby	1958	FC /FG
□ ○ **Toppers, Bobby Mitchell & the**	**One Friday Morning**	**1953**	**SP**
□ ○ Tops, Little Jimmy Rivers & the	Puppy Love	1961	FC
□ ○ **Tradewinds, Rudy & the**	**Careless Love**	**1962**	**SC**
□ ○ Treble Chords	Theresa	1959	FC
□ ○ Tremaines	Jingle Jingle	1958	FC
□ ○ **Tremaines**	**Moon Shining Bright**	**1958**	**SC**
□ ○ **Trend-Tones (aka Paradons)**	**Never Again**	**1961**	**SC**
□ ○ Triumphs, Tico & the	Cards Of Love	1963	FN
□ ○ Tru-Tones	Magic	1957	FC
□ ○ **Trueleers**	**Waiting For You**	**1963**	**SN/ FG**
□ ○ **Trueloves**	**A Love Like Yours**	**1957**	**FC**
□ ○ **Truetones**	**Honey Honey**	**1958**	**FC**
□ ○ Tune Weavers	Happy Happy Birthday Baby	1957	SC /FL
□ ○ **Tune Weavers, Margo Sylvia & the**	**Come Back To Me**	**1989**	**SC**

□○ **Tune Weavers,** Margo Sylvia & the	**What Are You Doing New Year's Eve**	**1989**	**SC**
□○ Turbans	When You Dance	1955	FC
□○ **Turbans**	**Let Me Show You (Around My Heart)**	**1955**	**SC**
□○ **Turbans**	**I'm Nobody's**	**1956**	**SC**
□○ Turbans	Congratulations	1957	SC
□○ Turbans	Valley Of Love	1957	SC
□○ Turks	Emily	1955	SP
□○ Tuxedos	Yes It's True	1960	SC
□○ **Twilighters**	**Please Tell Me You're Mine**	**1953**	**SC**
□○ Twilighters	Little Did I Dream	1955	SP
□○ **Twilighters, Tony & the**	**Be My Girl**	**1960**	**FN**
□○ **Tyce, Napoleon & group**	**Sitting Here**	**1960**	**SN**
□○ Tymes	So Much In Love	1963	MN
□○ **Tymes**	**Wonderful Wonderful**	**1963**	**SN**
□○ Tymes	Somewhere	1963	SN
□○ Tyson, Roy & group	Oh What A Night For Love	1963	FC

157

□○ **Unique Teens**	**Jeannie**	**1958**	**SC**
□○ Uniques	Do You Remember	1959	SN
□○ **Uniques**	**Silvery Moon**	**1963**	**SC**
□○ Universals	Again	1957	SC
□○ **Universals**	**Love Bound**	**1961**	**FN**
□○ **Universals**	**A Love Only You Can Give**	**1962**	**SN**
□○ **Untouchables**	**Lovely Dee**	**1961**	**FC**
□○ Utopians, Mike & the	Erlene	1958	FC
□○ **Utopians**	**Along My Lonely Way**	**1962**	**SN**
□○ Vacels (Ricky & the)	Lorraine	1962	SN
□○ Val-Chords	Candy Store Love	1957	FC
□○ **Valentines**	**Tonight Kathleen**	**1954**	**SC**
□○ Valentines	Lily Maebelle	1955	FC
□○ Valentines	Woo Woo Train	1955	FC
□○ Valentines	Nature's Creation	1956	SC
□○ Valentines	Don't Say Goodnight	1957	SC
□○ **Valentinos**	**Rendezvous With You**	**1993**	**FC**
□○ **Valentinos**	**Dee I**	**1993**	**SC**
□○ **Valentinos**	**I Miei Giorni Felici**	**1993**	**SC**

□○ **Valentinos**	**My Vow To You**	**1993**	**SC**
□○ **Valentinos**	**Dear Sonia**	**1993**	**SC**
□○ Valiants	This Is The Night	1957	SC
□○ Valrays	Yo Me Pregunto	1963	FN
□○ Van Dykes	Come On, Baby	1958	SC
□○ **Van Dykes**	**The Bells Are Ringing**	**1958**	**SC**
□○ Vanguards	Moonlight	1958	SC
□○ **Vel Aires, Donald Woods & the**	**Death Of An Angel**	**1955**	**SC**
□○ Vel-Tones	Now	1960	FC
□○ **Vel-Tones**	**A Fool Was I**	**1959**	**SC**
□○ **Vel-Tones**	**I Need You So**	**1960**	**SC/ FL**
□○ **Vells, Little Butchie & the**	**Please Tell The Angels**	**1959**	**SC**
□○ Velours	My Love Come Back	1956	SC
□○ Velours	Can I Come Over Tonight	1957	SC
□○ Velours	This Could Be The Night	1957	SC
□○ **Velvet Angels (aka Diablos)**	**I'm In Love**	**1964**	**FC**
□○ **Velvet Angels (aka Diablos)**	**Fools Rush In**	**1975**	**FC**

159

□○ Velvetones (A)	The Glory Of Love	1957	SC
□○ **Velvetones (B)**	**Two Hearts In Love**	**1958**	**SC**
□○ Velvets (A)	I	1953	SP
□○ **Velvets (A)**	**I Cried**	**1954**	**SP**
□○ Velvets (B)	Tonight (Could Be The Night)	1961	FN
□○ **Velvets (B)**	**Lana**	**1961**	**FN**
□○ **Vernalls**	**Why Can't You Be True**	**1958**	**FC**
□○ **Versatiles**	**Passing By**	**1958**	**FC**
□○ **Versatones**	**Bila**	**1958**	**FC**
□○ **Vibes**	**Darling**	**1957**	**SC**
□○ **Vibranaires**	**Doll Face**	**1954**	**SP**
□○ Videls	Be My Girl	1959	FN
□○ Videls	Mr. Lonely	1960	MN
□○ Videos	Trickle Trickle	1958	FC
□○ **Videos**	**Moonglow You Know**	**1958**	**SC**
□○ Viscaynes	Stop What You're Doing	1961	SC
□○ **Visions**	**Teenager's Life**	**1960**	**FN**
□○ **Visuals**	**Dreams Are For Fools**	**1959**	**FC**
□○ **Visuals**	**Submarine Race**	**1962**	**FN**
□○ **Vocal-Teens**	**Be A Slave**	**1958**	**FC**

□ ○ Vocaleers	Be True	1952	SP
□ ○ Vocaleers	It Is A Dream	1952	SP
□ ○ Vocaleers	I Walk Alone	1953	SP
□ ○ **Vocaleers**	**The Night Is Quiet**	**1960**	**SC**
□ ○ Voices	Two Things I Love	1955	FP
□ ○ Volumes	I Love You	1962	FN
□ ○ **Volumes**	**Dreams**	**1962**	**SC**
□ ○ Voxpoppers	Wishing For Your Love	1958	SC
□ ○ Wanderers	Thinking Of You	1957	SC
□ ○ **Wanderers**	**Great Jumpin' Catfish**	**1957**	**FC**
□ ○ Wheels	My Heart's Desire	1956	SC
□ ○ Whirlers	Magic Mirror	1956	SC
□ ○ **Whirlers**	**Tonight And Forever**	**1957**	**FC**
□ ○ **Whirlwinds**	**Heartbeat**	**1963**	**FN**
□ ○ Whispers	Fool Heart	1954	SP
□ ○ Willows	Church Bells May Ring	1956	FC
□ ○ **Willows**	**Now That I Have You**	**1961**	**SC**
□ ○ **Windsors, Lee Scott & the**	**My Gloria**	**1958**	**FC**
□ ○ **Wisdoms**	**Lost In Dreams**	**1959**	**FC**

□○ Wrens	Beggin' For Love	1955	SP
□○ Wrens	Come Back My Love	1955	FP
□○ **Wrens**	**Eleven Roses (And The Twelfth Is You)**	**1955**	**FC**
□○ Wrens	C'est La Vie	1956	SC
□○ **Young, Bobby & group**	**Only Girl For Me**	**1963**	**FN**
□○ **Young Lads**	**Moonlight**	**1956**	**SC**
□○ **Young Ones**	**Sweeter Than**	**1964**	**SC**
□○ **Young Ones**	**Mary Ann**	**1975**	**FC**
□○ Youngsters	Shattered Dreams	1956	FC
□○ **Zephyrs, Ben Joe Zeppa & the**	**Foolish Fool**	**1956**	**FC**
□○ **Zip, Danny & group**	**Hey Hey Girl**	**1964**	**FN**
□○ **Zircons**	**Lonely Way**	**1963**	**SC**
□○ **Zircons**	**Your Way**	**1963**	**SC**
□○ Zodiacs, Maurice Williams & the	Stay	1960	FC

Comparisons

When compiling the Top 1000 a few years ago, a con-certed effort was made to NOT have many versions of the same song, with a few exceptions. The thinking was that we wanted to include as wide a range of songs as we could and presenting multiple versions of, say, "Sunday Kind Of Love" would result in leaving out other tracks that deserved to be in-cluded.

By expanding to 2000 songs, we can include multiple versions of many songs, so that listeners can compare them for themselves. While there are far too many to list, we'll sug-gest some and let the reader find others. **Wherever the reader sees #1 below, it means that the song was in the first Top 1000. When #2 appears, it means the song was chosen for the second Top 1000 (making the Top 2000).**

A Story Untold (Here In My Heart Is...)

We begin with the Nutmegs classic grind "A Story Un-told," with Leroy Griffin' melismatic soulful lead in 1955 (#1). Then in 1961, the Time-Tones or Timetones (take your pick) put out a fast version (#1) with similar but not identical lyrics and a peppy danceable arrangement entitled "(Here) In My Heart." In 1963 the Emotions put out a mid-tempo cha-cha (#2), with lots of falsetto and bass, called "A Story Untold," but having lyrics and an arrangement more similar to the Time-tones fast version. Go figure.

A Thousand Stars

Gene Pearson led the Rivileers on this chestnut from 1954 (#1). In 1960, 15 year old Kathy Young led the Inno-cents in a sweet, soppy grindy remake (#2). Her voice is clear and young and, along with "Baby Oh Baby" by the Shells and "Angel Baby" by Rosie & the Originals (not doo-wop, merely uniwop) attracted a new generation of teens to our music, as did the "Oldies But Goodies" series of albums.

The Clock

Lee Andrews & the Hearts had the first of these, in 1957 (#1). Teddy & the Continentals remade the song with very few changes, the largest of which was in its title; i.e. "Tick Tick Tock" in 1961 (#2). Richie Cordell & group recorded "Tick Tock" in 1962 (#2) which is an entirely different song, as are songs entitled "The Clock" by the Jaytones in 1958 (ballad, #2) and the Contenders in 1963 (rocker, #1).

The Closer You Are

The standard here is the slow grind by Earl Lewis & the Channels in 1956 (#1). In 1961, a group called the Magnificent Four put out a fast version (#1), with a neo-doo-wop arrangement (lots of bass and nonsense syllables) that achieved some popularity in New York. A third version, by the Savoys, done acappella in 1965 (#2) is worth comparing. Though the Channels version is the standard, the other two have their own strengths.

Come Back My Love

Compare the Wrens popular version of "Come Back My Love" (#1) with the Cardinals equally competent version (#2), both out in 1955. Since the song was written by Bobby Mansfield, it is assumed that the Wrens took the first shot. But we're not done... there is a third version that will knock your socks off! Paul Himmelstein (schoolboy lead) fronted the Heartbreakers (#2) at a show at the Apollo (live) in an acappella effort that changes tempo from slow to fast about two-thirds of the way through the song. The audience was quite enthusiastic, as are we.

Crazy For You

Listen to the Aquatones 1960 sweet version (#2) of the Heartbeats 1956 classic (#1). Nothing can top that original, but Barbara Lee does a super job on lead.

Ding Dong Teenage Bells

Led by Dave Concepcion, the Five Secrets put out "Ding Dong Teenage Bells" in 1957 (#2). The group was also known as the Loungers and Secrets whose exact version of the same song, same arrangement came out on a different label in 1991. German groups have taken to this song like white on rice. In 1991, The Crystalairs put out "Ding Dong Teenage Bells" (#2), and in 1995 the Belangels (#2) did the same under the title "Teenage Bells" done in acappella style. The song lends itself to tight harmonies, pronounced contribution by the bass and frantic tempo. The Crystalairs slow down the song slightly, as do the Belangels. Both German groups are fantastic and both renditions are better than the one by the Five Secrets, if only because the tempo is easier on the ears.

Denise

Here's an interesting comparison. Listen to "Denise" by Randy & the Rainbows from 1963 (#1) and then play their followup, "Why Do Kids Grow Up," from later that same year (#2). They are almost identical in melody and tempo.

Don't Leave Me

The well-known version of this uptempo song is by the Magnificents in 1958 (#1). Compare it to the one done by the Continentals & the Counts of Rhythm, also in 1958 (#2). The Magnificents cut is superb and professional, with bass and background chanting "dun duh dun duh dun dooly wah" throughout most of the song. The Continentals version is not as polished but has interesting features. It begins slowly, with the lyrics, "Do you take this girl to be your wife. To fuss and fight for the rest of your life." The tempo then changes to upbeat, with the same "dun duh dun..." riff running underneath. The melody is not exactly the same as the Magnificents' version, and it's amateurish by comparison, but pleasing nonetheless.

Gee

Everyone knows the classic doo-wop by the Crows, put out in 1954 (#1). But listen to "Love Only You" by the Meadowlarks, also in 1954 (#2) which was their first recording. It's the exact cadence and melody, and the lyrics are pretty close. These days there would've been a law suit. Back then this semi-theft by a west coast group of an east coast hit probably wasn't discovered for years. Plus the Meadowlarks song didn't make much of a splash.

Gloria

This is the standard Leon Rene song that was "borrowed" and tweaked by Esther Navarro, manager of the Cadillacs. It's been recorded a host of times. Compare the following versions.

Four Gabriels	#2	1948
Cadillacs	#1	1954
Channels, Earl Lewis & the	#2	1956
Passions	#2	1960
Salutations, Vito & the	#2	1962
Darchaes, Nicky Addeo & the	#2	1963
Savoys	#2	1965

There are other great (but different) songs with "Gloria" in the title in our Top 2000. They are:

New Yorkers Five	Gloria, My Darling	#1	1955
Clefftones	Gloria	#2	1955
Crowns, A.L. Maye &	Gloria	#1	1956
Five Chances	Gloria	#1	1956
Windsors	My Gloria	#2	1958
Chariots	Gloria	#1	1959
Hi-Lites	Gloria (My Darling)	#1	1962
Fascinators	Gloria, My Love	#2	1996

Glory Of Love

Another standard redone by vocal groups, it was originally a number one hit for Benny Goodman with Helen Ward on vocals in 1936. The Five Keys had an R&B hit with it in 1951 (#1) replete with Rudy West's melismatic lead, falsetto over the lead, and blow harmonies. In 1955 the Platters (#2) came out with a poppish remake, featuring Tony Williams' smoothly crooned lead, Herb Reed's bass and Zola Taylor's sweet voice as part of the harmony.

The best version by far however, in our estimation, is that of the Velvetones in 1957 (#1). While the harmonizers sing the melody, the dramatic lead speaks almost throughout the whole song. He tells the story of having stuck by his girl who was working her way up the ladder to stardom and a "fine fine superfine career." He reads from three letters sent by her. The first shows her appreciation for his support, the second implies that success has gone to her head, and the third just says, "Please sign my check." He then calls her "You poor sad worthless foolish fool" and he realizes that he loves her much too much." Shakespeare within doo-wop!

The last two versions are also good, but not as good. The Roomates' track in 1961 (#2) features Steve Susskind's sweet nasal lead and perfect background harmony. And the Sharks Quintet replicated the Five Keys arrangement in 1974 (#2) with Buzzy Garland on lead and more of a bass part than the original.

Guardian Angel

The original version came out in 1958, by the Selections (#1) and was the only one included in the Top 1000. It was remade in 1961 by the Camerons (#2), who added a slow introduction ("Whenever I'm lonely, whenever I'm blue...") leading to a raucous, hand clapping version with honking sax. This group became the Demilles that put out "Donna Lee" (#1). The Imaginations also came out with a version that year (#2) featuring the great voice of Frank Mancuso and smooth harmonies by the background singers. This is our preference, but we do tolerate other opinions.

Nick Santo's Capris redid GA in 1982 (#2), as did the Legends of Doo-Wop (#2) in the late 1990s. Both of these versions are excellent. Santo intermixes a falsetto, adding a wrinkle to the standard arrangement. Frank Mancuso is on lead again for the Legends great version. But it's almost like cheating when you have Tony Passalacqua (Fascinators), Jimmy Gallagher (Passions) and Steve Horn (Five Sharks) as background singers.

But wait a minute! Thanks to YouTube (again), an unknown (at least to us) version appeared, one called "Bada Bada" by the Princetones (#2) (purported to be an early version of the Bon-Aires) which is 90% the same song. It is apparently a demo recorded at Allegro Sound Studios on Broadway in New York City and has a handwritten date of 4/16/58. It is likely that this was copied by the Selections; less likely that the Princetones heard the Selections version and toyed with the song as a demo.

Notes: The development of the second thousand best songs allowed the addition of five versions to compare with the Selections output, which was the only one included in the Top 1000. Readers should note that the flip of the Selections version is "Soft And Sweet" (#2), which itself can be compared to the beautiful version by the Continentals (#1) from 1956.

Heart And Soul

Compare the 1951 bass-led (Tommy Smith doing his best Jimmy Ricks impersonation) paleo-doo-wop version (#2) by the Four Buddies to the neo-doo-wop 1961 track by the Herb Cox led Cleftones (#1). If there was ever a clear example of the difference between the paleo- and neo- eras, this is it.

Hearts Of Stone

Compare the original of this song by the Jewels in 1954 (#1) to the cover by Otis Williams & the Charms later in the year (#2). Both are good. This song was covered by several white groups and became a pop hit. The Jewels came out with a sequel, "Hearts Can Be Broken" in 1955 (#2) which has al-most an identical sound.

He's/She's Gone
Compare the Chantels "He's Gone" (#1) from 1957 with "She's Gone" (#2) by the Carians in 1961.

I Cried
In 1953, Bobby Mitchell & the Toppers, put out a song called "One Friday Morning" (#2). The style is New Orleans bluesy with a heavy piano in the background. The central lyrics are "I cried, I cried, I lied, I lied." The next year, the Velvets put out a New York style, doo-woppy ballad under the title, "I Cried." Very similar lyrics, very similar melody. Did someone hear the Toppers track and give it a little twist? You tell us...

I Only Want You
This was the B-side of the great ballad "This Is My Love" by the Passions in 1960 (#1). The Legends of Doo-Wop reprised "I Only Want You" (as well as the flip) in 1998 (#2). The Fabulons, a Queens, NY group, did a good version in 1961 (#2). And Richie & the Royals did an even better acappella version in 1963 (#2). Great song, no matter who does it.
Speaking of acappella and the Passions, the Young Ones did a super acappella remake of the Passions' "This Is My Love" in 1964, but retitled it "Sweeter Than" (#2).

I Promise To Remember
Jimmy Castor, schoolboy lead of the Juniors (Jimmy Cas-tor & the Juniors) wrote this song in 1956 (#2). Frankie Lymon & the Teenagers (#1) quickly covered it in the same year and had the more popular (by far) version. Castor and Lymon went to the same school in Harlem, NY. The Juniors' version fea-tures a wonderful bass riff, "Doom doom, mick doom doom, mick doom doom, mick doom" which appears in the intro, the bridge and the end of the song and sets it apart, though the Teenagers' rendition was recorded more professionally.

I Sold My Heart To The Junkman

There are three versions of this standard in the Top 2000, co-written by Leon Rene (the composer of the original "Gloria"). The first is by the Los Angeles based Basin Street Boys, recorded in 1946 (#2), the second is by the Silhouettes in 1958 (#1) and the last is by the female group, the (Patti La-Belle) Blue Belles in 1962 (#2). The Basin Street version is sweet and slow, with blow harmonies under Ormande Wilson's lead. The Silhouettes version is "doo-wopped up," replete with "bop bop bop" background and is slightly faster.

The Blue Belles version is from another planet. First of all, it is thought that either the song was performed by a totally different group, called the Starlets, or by the Blue Belles under the name "Starlets." In any case, it appears on various Blue Belles CDs. It's a true 1960s girl group sound, uptempo, violins in the background, doo-wop harmonies and LaBelle's stratospheric lead voice. Don't play it anywhere near good stemwear.

I Wonder Why

Another first-as-best case. The 1958 release of "I Wonder Why" (#1) by Dion & the Belmonts put the white group sound on the map. Carlo Mastrangelo's machine gun bass ("dun dun dun, duh dun duh dun dun, duh duh dun dun dun, duh dun duh duh duh duh duh duh"), Dion's crooning lead and tight background harmonies make this perhaps the favorite uptempo doo-wop of all time. It simply can't be beat.

The Chiffons put out a nice version in 1963 (#2) with sweet vocals, but Carlo's bass "dun dun dun..." intro is replaced by a tinny guitar which stinks (in our opinion). The German group, the Crystalairs put out a version in 1991 entitled "Frag' Nicht Warum" (#2), which is German for "Do Not Ask Why" but is the exact same song. Their voices are good, the harmony tight and the arrangement precise. Great array of nonsense syllables and creative use of falsetto.

The last version included in the Top 2000 is a live version recorded in 1972 at a Richard Nader concert (#2). Nader announces, "From our very first Rock 'n' Roll Revival, I must've received a hundred, 200, 300 letters every single show saying can't you get Dion and the Belmonts back together?! Dion said yes! The Belmonts said yes! Ladies and gentlemen, Dion & the Belmonts!" And then the song launches with Carlo's bass... Dion is in great voice and changes the melody of the song slightly, to great effect. Worth finding and listening to...

I'm So Happy

Compare Lewis Lymon & the Teenchords version from 1957 (#1) with the one produced by Phil Spector for the Ducanes in 1961 (#2). The latter has a frantic pace, falsetto lead and a "yeller" in the bridge.

Little Girl Of Mine

Compare the popular Cleftones track from 1956 (#1) with the cover by the Hurricanes, also in 1956 (#2). Cleftones lead is better, but the bass play on the Hurricanes record is very interesting ("Yay-yuh"). We call it a draw.

Love No One But You

The original version, by the Jesters in 1957 (#1), is by far the best. In fact slow doo-wop doesn't get any better than this song. Incidentally, original versions are usually hard to beat. Our ears get used to the original and it's difficult to think of a cover or remake as better. Different maybe, but not better.

The Excellents, from the Bronx, gave it a good try in 1961 (#2) and the Five Chancells did a capable acappella version in 1965, but both efforts just point out the unparalleled quality of the original.

There's a little irony here. The Diablos recorded "The Wind" in 1954 (#1) featuring the incomparable tenor lead of Nolan Strong. The Jesters remade the song in 1960 (#2), and though technically close to perfect, can't match the emotional valence of Strong's original.

Having said that, there's another comparison that contradicts the first-as-best rule. The Swallows recorded "I Only Have Eyes For You" in 1952 (#2). The song is a standard, having been written in 1934 by Harry Warren and Al Dubin for a movie featuring Dick Powell and Ruby Keeler. Their rendition was sweet and soulful, as was the Swallows' wont, and it attracted exactly no attention. Zero. Seven years later, in 1959, the Flamingos remade the same tune (#1), featuring a reverberation effect to create an ethereal atmosphere, and that contained classy harmonies by one of the most talented vocal groups of all time.

Maybe You'll Be There

Lee Andrews & the Hearts recorded this standard (written in 1947) in 1954 as a ballad (#1), the way it was originally intended. Billy & the Essentials sped it up for a bouncy version in 1962 (#1). Also in 1962 the Hi-Lites (#2) added their own wrinkles (bass, slight change in lyrics) and slowed it down again.

Please Say You Want Me

Everyone knows the original, by the Leslie Martin led Schoolboys in 1957 (#1). The Cleftones remade it in 1961, with Pat Spann (female) replacing Martin's kiddie lead. Good job.

Sticking with the Cleftones, compare their original version of "You Baby You" from 1956 (#1) with the excellent bass-laden remake by the Excellents in 1962 (#2). Most of the melody is carried by falsetto-topped harmonizers. Faster, different than the Cleftones, but just as good.

So Tough

The first version of this song was put out by the Houston, TX group the Casuals (aka Original Casuals) on Back Beat in 1957 (#2). Gary Mears was the lead singer and wrote the song. There are two other versions by two other groups whose names are homonyms; the Kuf-Linx on Challenge in 1958 (#1) and the Cuff Links also in 1958 (#2) on Dootone. The last two sound very different despite the similarity in names.

Stars In The Sky

Earl Lewis & the Channels did the signature version of this in 1956 (#2). The (black) Mystics did a remake in 1962

(#2) that, though not as good, is interesting in and of itself. What do you think?

Note: the Chanters (#2) recorded a track with the same name in 1958 but it is a different song.

Stormy Weather

Written in 1933 by Harold Arlen and Ted Koehler, "Stormy Weather" was first recorded by Ethel Waters and then by everyone else who was anyone. The first doo-wop recording was by the Five Sharps in 1952, and the origin and subsequent events that befell this version are too complicated to cite her, but as a tease the tale involves the differing stories of many people, Slim Rose of Times Square records and Teddy, his pet raccoon. (Yes, raccoon.) The unabridged story can be found in "The Complete Book of Doo-Wop" by Gribin and Schiff (2000) under the heading "Stormy Whether."

The Five Sharps hailed from Queens, NY, and their version (#1) contains the sound effects of thunder and rain, a tinkly piano intro and a soulful delivery by Ronald Cuffey. The group wasn't together for long, but most members went on to sing with other groups such as the Videos and Shep & the Limelights. As a record it is about as rare as they come, at least in its original form.

The Leaders put out a good but quirky version in 1955 (#1). "The last pork chops I had taste like leather," "why momma won't bake no apple pie; starvation; since I lost my profession." As we said, quirky, but interesting. Then in 1958, Pookie Hudson's Spaniels (#1) sped it up and gave us another classic. All three differ and are worth a tumble.

Stranded In The Jungle/Church Bells May Ring

The Jayhawks were out first with "Stranded…" in 1956 (#1), which was rapidly covered and outsold by the Cadets, another west coast group in 1957 (#1). The Cadets version is more professionally done; the Jayhawks more streetcornerish. The Cadets (#2) recidivated by covering the 1956 Willows' "Church Bells May Ring" (#1) in the same year. A version by

173

the Diamonds, a cover group that was white and sounded it, outsold both of them on Mercury.

Sunday Kind Of Love

This song is so famous that it has its own wikipedia entry. It was written by four people including Louis Prima in 1946 and has been recorded countless times. There were two versions in the Top 1000, one slow and one fast. The slow version was by Willie Winfield & the Harptones (#1) in 1953; the fast was by the Del Vikings (#1) in 1957. These are paragons for slow and fast versions, respectively.

Nine versions were added for the Top 2000. They are:

Kings, Bobby Hall & the	1953	#2	SP

Baltimore group that came out with this a few months after the Harptones.

Sentimentals	1957	#2	FC

Light uptempo version

Marcels	1961	#2	SC

Classical doo-wop version, including great bass by Fred Johnson and significant background harmony in play.

Heard, Lonnie (bb/5 Dollars)	1961	#2	FN

Quirky poppish version, with good background by an ex perienced group.

Roommates (A)	1962	#2	SC

Sweet white sound, Steve Susskind on lead. Typical pleasing Roomates effort.

Excellons	1961	#2	FN

Really the Excellents in Excellons clothing. Great version, lots of bass, done acappella.

Devotions	1964	#2	FN

Starts slow, delaying the pace change, speeds up pleasantly. Rip Van Winkle bass is good.

TimeTones	1964	#2	FC

Another fine acappella effort from the Times Square stable.

Del Chateaus	1964	#2	FN

Starts very slow like the Devotions version, then turns frantic. Nasal lead, pleasing result.

Note: The Harptones slow version was first turned fast by the Del Vikings and most versions since then have been up-tempo. The simple (but artful) melody lends itself to the nonsense syllables, bass and background harmonies of doo-wop. Slow versions require a great lead, such as Willie Winfield, or in the pop world, Fran Warren or Jo Stafford.

The Top 2000 allows comparison between and among all the versions. Each one adds a new wrinkle to the original slow or fast version. We could've included many more in our list.

Teenager's Dream/Dreams Come True

The Pearl McKinnon Kodaks put out a beautiful sentimental ballad called Teenager's Dream in 1957 (#1). The Earls sped up the song to a lindy tempo and put it out as "Dreams Come True" in 1973 (#2). The two songs sound totally different, despite having almost the same exact lyrics and melody.

While we're on the Earls, they also sped up the classic "Life Is But A Dream" by the Harptones from 1954 (#1) to produce the first of their nonsense syllable-laden efforts that made one want to dance and sing along in 1961 (#1). Witness "Dang dang bop bop a shoo bop duh bop bop." And the reader should compare their "Never" from 1963 (#1) to a version in Spanish entitled "Nunca," (which means "Never" in Spanish) by Julito & the Latin Lads from the same year (#2).

Tell My Why

The original, by Norman Fox & the Rob Roys in 1957 (#1), is considered one of the best uptempo doo-wops ever recorded. It's all there... progressive voice entrances, nonsense syllables (chop chop chop chop), bass punctuation, falsetto trail off... the whole shebang! The Belmonts (sans Dion) redid it in 1961 (#2), rearranged it slightly and did it credit. We especially like the trailoff by Carlo Mastrangelo with, "Dun, dun duh dun dun, dun duh dun dun, dun dun duh duh duh duh duh duh duh..."

That's My Desire

This song from 1931 has been recorded hundreds of times. We include four doo-wop versions, each in a different style. Earl Lewis & the Channels recorded the most well-known version in 1957 (#1) done in classical doo-wop style. The harmonizers carry the melody and Earl Lewis' soaring falsetto wanders above them, then Lewis takes over the lead in the bridge.

Four years previously, in 1953, Sollie McElroy led the Flamingos (#2) in a bluesy, sensuous version, paleo-doo-wop style, that features a soft sax in the background and an occasional falsetto over the melody.

1957 saw another paleo-version by the Chuck Carbo-led Spiders (#1). Goosing the tempo slightly, putting in a back beat, and having the harmonizers chant "doo-wadda doo-wadda doo-wop" makes for an interesting and different effort.

Finally in 1960, Dion & the Belmonts put the song out as the B-side of "Where Or When" (#2). They go back to Channels arrangement, with harmonizers on lead and falsetto above. The perfect harmony and Dion's beautiful nasality (if nasality can be beautiful) makes this version the equal of the Channels'. Four different, worthwhile tracks.

Them There Eyes

In 1930, the mother of the first author (Doris Tauber Gribin) wrote the melody to a standard called "Them There

Eyes." The lyrics were written by William Tracey, and the title coined by Maceo Pinkard, better known for his song "Sweet Georgia Brown." The song was recorded first by Bing Crosby & the Rhythm Boys, then by Louis Armstrong, Duke Ellington, Billie Holiday, Frank Sinatra, Ella Fitzgerald and everybody else that was anybody through the years. There are over 500 versions extant. It has crossed genres, going from the pop world, to the blues, to big band, to gypsy jazz to dixieland to rock 'n' roll.

There are three versions in the Top 2000. The first was by Lewis Lymon & the Teenchords in 1958 (#2) as the flip of "Dance Girl" (#2). The second was by a female group called the Chic Chocs with an early girl group sound recorded in 1961 (#2). The last and, we believe by far the best, was an after-era rendition by Norman Smith's Keystoners from Philadelphia in 1993 (#2).

Yo Me Pregunto

Compare the two versions of "Yo Me Pregunto," which means "I Wonder." Both are sung in Spanish and are catchy bouncy takes on the same tune. The Valrays version was recorded in 1963 (#1) and Concepts' acappella version came out in 1966 (#2). Both are good. By the way, the composers are listed as "Linda/Antrell." Any relation to Dave Antrell, the first Doctor of Doo-Wop?

Zoom Zoom Zoom

The Collegians have the first and preeminent version, released in 1957 (#1). Hard drumbeat start, then the bass enters: "Bon bon, buh bon buh bon bon, buh buh bon bon bon, buh bon buh bon bon bon..." Seminal recording, and one that provided the inspiration for Fred Johnson's famous riff on "Blue Moon" by the Marcels in 1961. For those of you into the Marcels, listen to their audition song "Zoom" (#2). It's not "Zoom Zoom Zoom," but it combines elements of "Zing Went The Strings Of My Heart" by the Coasters (#2) and their own "Blue Moon" (#1).

177

Turning to the comparison versions, the Enchords in 1961 (#2) do a capable job on the song, but there is some sort of mellow brass instrument (trumpet or sax?) running behind the harmonizers throughout the song that adds a nice twist. It's almost a countermelody. The Dreamlovers put out a version in 1962 (#2) featuring a nice lead and a slightly changed base line which includes a trill. And the Hi-Lites in 1962 (#2) add wrinkles by changing the melody slightly and amending the bass line to: "Bow bow buh bow buh bow bow, diddly bow, mem mem mem muh mem..." For those readers who are into bass riffs, this is a special treat.

Zoop

The original was done by the Charts in 1957 (#1) as the flip of their grindy romantic oeuvre "Desirie." In 1962 the HI-Lites put their own spin on it (#2), with a new arrangement and lots of bass to produce a sound just as good as the original. Compare both of these with a song called "And When I'm Near You" by Richie & the Royals in 1961 (#1). It's close to the same song. Both begin with something akin to "zoom de dah de dah zoom bop bah..." but then diverge slightly. The Charts sing "zoop zoop zoop be doop" while the Royals chant "zoop zoop zoop wee oop." Trivial yet profound.

www.ingramcontent.com/pod-product-compliance
Lightning Source LLC
Chambersburg PA
CBHW022022090426

42739CB00006BA/245